C000277911

A BORDERLINE CASE

JERRY GALVIN

Grosvenor House
Publishing Limited

All rights reserved
Copyright © Jerry Galvin, 2022

The right of Jerry Galvin to be identified as the author of this
work has been asserted in accordance with Section 78
of the Copyright, Designs and Patents Act 1988

The book cover is copyright to Jerry Galvin

This book is published by
Grosvenor House Publishing Ltd
Link House
140 The Broadway, Tolworth, Surrey, KT6 7HT.
www.grosvenorhousepublishing.co.uk

This book is sold subject to the conditions that it shall not, by way of
trade or otherwise, be lent, resold, hired out or otherwise circulated
without the author's or publisher's prior consent in any form of binding or
cover other than that in which it is published and
without a similar condition including this condition being imposed
on the subsequent purchaser.

A CIP record for this book
is available from the British Library

ISBN 978-1-80381-167-3

DEDICATION

This is dedicated to my parents and the border,
without which these wayward scribbles
would not have been possible.

Patrick and Jenny Galvin

Thankful gratitude to Ellie Beale, my long-suffering granddaughter who typed this tome from dictation and who now knows more of Clones than she ever dreamed of.

With appreciation also to Laura Morgan who in her garden shed "study" turned this somewhat rambling manuscript into something resembling a book.

For Meg McGowan

Driving Ulster's border, the latter end of June
Solstice sunset, languid, long, a hanging harvest moon
Roadside verges shimmer, hawthorn hedgerows lush
The duet of the dying day, a blackbird and a thrush
Ballyshannon to Belleek, Rossinver to Belcoo
By garrison and kilty a rising Melvin dew
Kilometres in Donegal, Fermanagh runs on mileage
Meadows mown and all bailed up in black plastic, silage
Ocean breezes bending boughs of conifer and birch
Keening swallows skim and wheel o'er Cashel's parish church
Under Sean McDermott's sky little did he know
When he faced Kilmainham's firing squad all those years ago
A landline skirts his birthplace, of bitterness and strife
Was it really worth it all for such a noble life?

IN THE BEGINNING

The *London Times* of 12 December 1942, a typical wartime edition, is a usual miscellany of the serious and the mundane.

In war reportage, Rommel, "the desert fox", was defeated at El Alamein. Montgomery and his battle-hardened "D-Day dodgers" were now turning their sound-blasted tank turrets towards Anzio Salerno and Monte Casino. The siege of Stalingrad collapses through a combination of Russian and winter grit; the Third Reich is imploding.

In the shopping post section, carrots (selected table) can be purchased for eight shillings and sixpence per sack… same quality as last year. A long-sleeved wool dress (second-hand, originally expensive) is for sale… contact box number 5/1462. Due to a briar shortage, pipe smokers are encouraged to have their pipes hygienically cleaned in what must have been the first smoking warning, the procedure carried out by Astley's of Jermyn Street, London, W1 for the princely sum of two shillings.

In the nuptials column, Sir Patrick Heron-Maxwell has been joined in matrimony to Miss D.C.E. Paget-Mellor at Holy Trinity Church, Richmond, Surrey (whatever will they call the children?).

Noël Coward's *Blithe Spirit* is having an extended run at the Duchess Theatre, Catherine Street, WC2.

On the trading markets, the price of wheat (English milled) is selling at 73 shillings and sixpence per hundredweight… farm price wholesale… To purchase the same from merchants, 74 shillings and seven and a half pence.

The battlefield casualty section is a roll call in honour of the following: missing, believed killed in action.

As a very minor footnote in history, on this day, sometime in the late afternoon or early evening, I was safely delivered into the loving, comforting warm arms of my mother.

Roots

I was born in the village of Clones (pronounced clo-ness) in the County of Monaghan and one mile from an empire at war. The first generation of a New Ireland and 20 years of independence. Monaghan, translated from Gaelic, means the county of little hills, and so it was, a mini verdant Alps of rolling hillocks, interspersed with meandering streams and reed-ringed lakes. These lakelets teemed with pike, perch, tench and roach where wild ducks left chevron ripples and water hens scampered across pink-flowered lilies. Along their course, these brooks tumbled over beaver dams into placid rock pools where the brown trout rose to the morning mayfly. These tributaries emptied into the larger River Finn, in turn emptying into Lough Erne, and eventually into the Atlantic Ocean.

Majestic Lough Erne

Originally one of the nine counties of old Ulster, it was on partition, together with the counties of Cavan and Donegal, jettisoned off into the new Republic. These counties, with overwhelming Catholic majorities, would ensure the remaining six would become, in the words of Lord Carson, "a Protestant state for Protestant people". The county was mainly agricultural, mostly small holdings with clusters of threepenny-stamp-sized fields. Rising and falling, they were enclosed by hawthorn hedgerows interwoven with sally saplings. In springtime, on the mossy banks beneath, wild primroses and bluebells peeped out in perfusion. Dotted around the pinnacles, here a wild furze, there a sloe bush and perfumed heather. Low-lying meadows were soggy and rushy, the bog cotton gliding in the breeze.

A panoramic view over Clones

Even though now a pariah county, Monaghan's many acres still provided an industrial umbilical cord to the Belfast textile trade. As the main grower of flax, it provided raw material for the city's linen mills. With Belfast climatic conditions ideal, these wonderful, delicate fibres were woven into a world-renowned product. Crisp sheets and pillowcases, fitted on the beds in the luxury suites of the world's top hotels, guaranteed cooling comfort in summer and snug slumber in winter. The dinner tables of London society soirées and England's stately homes were adorned and embellished with tablecloths and napkins spun by the side of the River Lagan in the Laganside mills, but whose origins were cultivated in the "stony grey hills of Monaghan".

3

My Parents

If the partition of Ireland stood for division and dissent, it's more than ironic that it was also responsible for the marital union of my parents and at very frequent intervals thereafter the arrival of my siblings and me.

My father, Patrick Joseph Galvin, hailed from the seaside resort of Ballybunion in the flatlands of northwest Kerry. Unlike Bundoran, sheltered in the lee of Donegal Bay, Ballybunion, lying at the southern tip of the Shannon Estuary, faced the full force of the Atlantic and the benign surges of the Gulf Stream.

Ballybunion's main claim to fame was its Islamic-style gender separated beaches, where a protruding cake slice cliff conveniently divided the town's golden strand. This natural divide was regarded by the local clergy as divine intervention. In a combination of Victorian prudery and Catholic moral teaching, Ballybunion's beach was frequently patrolled by the local parish priest to enforce this bathing apartheid. Even to this very day, both beaches are still referred to as the Lady's Strand and the Gent's Strand.

Born in 1895 in the reign of Queen Victoria, empress of India, defender of the faith and titular head of the British Empire, my father's life would span Irish independence and two world wars. Marrying late, as was the fashion of the day, he would be 47 years old when I was born, our two generations spanning three centuries.

His father, John Brendan Galvin, was born just after the famine in 1852. A cooper by trade, his work binding tempered hoops to barrels and cartwheels, was both skillful and labour intensive. Living until 1928, his longevity witnessed successive historic upheavals.

The issue of my grandfather's second marriage, my father grew up in a rural, simplistic Catholic Ireland. Education was basic: the three Rs, courtesy of Britain at the peak of its imperial power. By a combination of self-learning and determination, he joined the Royal Irish Constabulary, the pre-independence police force. His one and only posting to the Tipperary village of Killenaule was short but eventful. With the War of Independence in full vigour and the atmosphere febrile, intimidation was rife. Forced out of uniform by the IRA threat to torch the Ballybunion homestead, all he could do was lie

4

low and bide his time. In the scramble for jobs, the administration of the "ancien regime" was subsumed into the Irish Free State. My father managed to assimilate into the new Customs and Excise; the old cap badge of the royal crown was now replaced by the Irish harp. Initially, a temporary sinecure and working at the Customs House by the Liffeyside, he was about to become part of rapidly evolving events. In the first opening salvo of the Irish Civil War, the anti-treaty rebels proceeded to burn down the Forecourts and the Customs House. Escaping by good fortune, suffering superficial burns, he was despatched to the newly formed border. Starting along the Donegal/Derry sector, he worked along its entirety, finally procuring a permanent posting in Monaghan.

Tall and erect with a military bearing from his RIC days, which enhanced both his uniform and air of authority, his soft, lilting Kerry accent contrasted starkly with the flat, staccato clipped vowels of Ulster. He had to master very quickly the subtle coded words of everyday conversation, denoting religious affiliations. A consummate diplomat, all confidences were just that. Coming from the other end of the island, all the trappings of local bigotry were anathema to him. Ironically, most of his friends would be cross-border Protestant farmers, who in his words, "said what they did and did what they said" and supplied our house with constant largesse. My mother was inundated with bags of vegetables and orchard fruit of every kind. The bog where we cut our turf was freely provided by a Mr Morton, a Protestant small holder either for a favour received, or the turning of a Nelsonian blind eye.

The romantic setting for my parent's courtship was the hamlet of Garrison in County Fermanagh. My father, still on the move, was posted to the County Leitrim village of Kiltyclogher. This cockpit quadrangle of Counties Fermanagh, Leitrim, Donegal and Sligo was one of stunning beauty. Bisected by both Lough Melvin and Lough Erne and encircled by the low Sligo/Leitrim mountains, it was an area of haunting names... Glencar, Rossinver, Dromahair, Belleek, Belcoo and Derrylin.

My mother's elder sister, Minnie, was married to Jack McGowan, a rural retailer and the proprietor of Garrison's crossroads shop. This was an eclectic emporium in its own right, and where Jack was simultaneously a greengrocer, confectioner, supplier of paraffin fuel,

5

meal and flour, hardware and petrol. Also included in his portfolio was the solemn task of burying the dead. During the long winter evenings, the McGowan kitchen and parlour would transform into a "rambling house", where neighbours congregated for self-entertainment. My father would have cycled a mile or two between both jurisdictions. An object of curiosity, his soft Kerry brogue lilting and falling in contrast to the local dialect of Fermanagh. Before a blazing turf fire, the kitchen hummed to low talk of local gossip amid musical instruments accompanied by solo balladeers. On the linoleum floor, dancers performed jigs and reels. The local seanchaí would enthrall the children spellbound with tales of heroic deeds by Celtic warriors. My father, a poetry aficionado, would render his pièce de résistance, reciting Oliver Goldsmith's "The Deserted Village" in its entirety. In the parlour, card players were offered pyramid plates of sandwiches and endless cups of tea. It was on such an occasion that my mother, visiting her sister, would encounter and engage in an awkward shy dialogue with the new Customs man from Kiltyclogher.

McGowan Homestead at Cashel
where Cupid fired his Victorian dart!

Jenny Patricia Jordan was born in 1901 at the end of Victoria's reign and the cusp of a new century. Her mother, Margaret Gorman, came from the village of Kinlough, just on the Leitrim hinterland. Her brothers, jobbing builders, constructed a clutch of small boarding houses to capitalise on Bundoran as a burgeoning resort. One of these, my mother's birthplace, would have been offered as a bricks and mortar dowry. My maternal grandfather, Henry Jordan, arrived in Bundoran as station master. A Belfast Protestant, he converted to the Church of Rome on his marriage to Margaret, an occurrence of its time so unique as to be incredible. If the Queen's blood is "blue", my lineage would suggest a fusion of green and orange. My mother's siblings were an all-girl family, save for my uncle Jack, a Wicklow policeman, who was hilariously funny and the life and soul of every party. Here in the bustling summer kitchen of Antrim House, the Jordan girls honed their domestic skills as future homemakers themselves. A daily communicant, with a laid-back easygoing way, an infectious smile, raucous laugh and twinkling eyes, Jenny Jordan was the family peacemaker, summoned frequently for family feuds and divisions.

Following the initial encounter in the convivial atmosphere of Garrison, a long-distance courtship followed, as my father moved from custom post to custom post, and cordial relations were maintained by stamp and envelope. Following the prospect of a permanent posting in Clones, Patrick Joseph Galvin and Jenny Patricia Jordan became man and wife in 1934. As with the social norms of the day, my parents married late with my father aged 39 and my mother slightly younger.

With the biological clock running fast, babies arrived at almost nine-monthly intervals. First came Peggie, then Eileen, John, Harry (who died in infancy) and I finally completed the brood in 1942.

O'NEILL PARK

Our first family abode was in the town's only housing estate... O'Neill Park. With 118 dwellings, it wound its way like a concrete necklace around the other main Appian hill and within decibel distance of the church. Most buildings were, in Pete Seeger's words, little boxes... basic, practical and bog standard, and where architectural inspiration was minimal.

O'Neill Park with millennium trappings

Each house comprised a thrupenny bit front lawn, a one-step porch leading to a three-step parlour-cum-living-room. At the rear was a pantry/kitchen/scullery with a deep Belfast sink, the glazed edge worn down by knife sharpening. Upstairs, three miniscule bedrooms put cat swinging out of the question. In the cluttered living room where my father's sturdy Raleigh bicycle took pride of place, a large cast metal range provided hot water, heating and food.

A recessed toilet was just outside the back door but just inside the backyard. Toilet paper was an original recycling concept, newspaper pages cut into sizeable squares, punched and dangling on a string. The back garden, some 60 by 30 foot, was of poor-quality soil, the residue of the foundations sticky and clawing. Over the years, my father would painstakingly enrich and cultivate the soil with layers of manure.

15 O'Neill Park – from Bakelite wireless to satellite dish

O'Neill Park tenants were of every social hue… policemen, customs men, tradesmen, shopkeepers, teachers, both the unemployed and the unemployable all living cheek by jowl. However, 18 houses stood apart from the rest of the total stock and would be described in estate agent jargon as the "crème de la crème". This row of terraced houses standing in line fronted the lower end of the estate, with panoramic views across the station and the town below. They also offered the "extra must-haves"… a separate parlour, and would you believe… a bathroom!

In the prehistoric days before health and safety and planning permission, cottage industries sprang up throughout the estate. One widow supplemented a meagre pension and transformed her living room into a confectionery emporium. Next door, an entrepreneurial baker in a rear outhouse produced pastries, bread and apple turnovers on par with any French patisserie. An elderly couple on the higher end of the estate geographically, but lower socially, entered the hospitality sector, offering short- and long-term accommodation. Their clientele included vagrants, beggars, fair day street performers and cattle dealers. To maximise limited space, total strangers huddled together for warmth with fleas and bedbugs as alarm clocks. Washing was by way of carbolic soap, ice water and frayed communal towels. Breakfast could only be described as continental: thick wedges of bread laced with margarine and homemade jam washed down with steamy porringers of tea and cocoa.

The swanky 18 row

We scholars at the nearby Largy National School treated the winding streets of O'Neill Park and the surrounding countryside as one giant playground. Living all together, then, in a total Irish monoculture, our street neighbours were like one enlarged family. We climbed trees, jumped across rivers and bogholes, we swam in the local lakes and dammed up rivers. We "progged" apples, pears and plums from the best orchards and nimbly picked gooseberries through thorny drenched bushes. We ran barefoot in the summer, our soles hardened by gravel roads and stained with melting tar. In winter, we manufactured our own ice rinks, pouring buckets of water on sloping streets.

With Brylcreem quiffs and scrubbed faces, we knelt on hard marble altar steps in cold churches, clad in starched white surplices and long black soutanes, chanting, in parrot fashion, the liturgical responses of the Tridentine Mass.

Seats Of Learning

In September 1946, just shy of my fourth birthday, I trooped off to the local infant school halfway down Church Hill and just above St Joseph's Hall. My first rite of passage, my mother stood on the topmost step of our hall door with arms folded and tears welling up and gently fondled my slicked-back hair, checking my brand-new shirt, shorts, socks and shoes. Hopping and skipping hand in hand with an older neighbour, Josie Hanna, I was placed in "loco parentis" of the St Louis nuns. My first impression of my would-be teachers was both ominous and menacing, draped, as they were, from head to toe in a shapeless black habit, their exposed faces enclosed by a picture portrait frame.

Any residue of maternal instinct must have long been dissipated by Catholic zealotry and a cloistered life, as, after a week, the nuns discovered I suffered from a serious physical disability… I was left-handed. Left-handedness, associated with mediaeval sorcery and shunned as the hand of the Devil, also got a bad rap in the gospels, where Jesus, having ascended into Heaven, sits on the right hand of the Father. Dying on the cross, Jesus forgave the repentant thief on his right. In some cultures and religions, the left hand was demoted to toiletry purposes only. It even has its own name in Gaelic… ciotóg (kithogue). To overcome this mistake by God, my left hand was summarily tied behind my back with a piece of string in order to write properly. However, with the nuns distracted, I would slip my leash and revert to type, pushing the nib pen against the grain along my lined exercise book, resulting in many blotched errors.

On the other hand, these "brides of Christ", unencumbered by marriage or family, were both focused and dedicated in their daily interaction in the classroom and away from the rigours of convent life. Our infant classrooms were sparsely furnished. We sat along wooden benches with intermittent recessed inkwells and packed tightly together. Standing in one corner, a large abacus, the Stone Age computer, in the other, a large blackboard on a swivel with a large piece of chalk dangling on a string. Daylight streamed through long, rectangular ecclesiastical windows. Nuns glided around the classrooms with swishing habits and long black rosaries dangling and clicking from

11

waist to hem. Walls and window ledges were adorned with various assorted pictures and statues of St Patrick, St Brigid, the Virgin Mary, St Francis of Assisi and the priest of Stigmata, Padre Pio.

In between the abacus and the alphabet, we boys with fringes, snotty noses, Fair Isle jumpers and rash-inducing short trousers, together with girls in ribbons and cotton frocks, skipped and hopscotched around our playground with joie de vivre.

National School

This was where our formal education commenced, now gender separated, as the girls remained under the tutelage of the nuns. We boys transferred to the Largy School and the care of the four masters... Masters Maguire, Kennedy, McCague and Kirke. National school was where we were introduced to the four Rs, the fourth being Religion.

Although freedom of religion was enshrined in the national constitution, successive Irish governments were virtual theocracies. Short of being a state-funded religion, the biggest subsidy by a Catholic government was to place the total education system in the gift of the Catholic Church. This ensured that Catholic indoctrination by nuns, priests and Christian brothers was complete. In the post-nationalistic fervour, the New Ireland would be distinctly Celtic, Irish speaking and monocultural. It would also be distinctively Catholic in contrast to English Protestantism, seen in Irish colonial eyes as heretical and created on a whim by a monarch in pursuit of a male heir.

The other irony was that the first official language of the Irish constitution wasn't the everyday language of the majority of its citizens. By choice, English was the lingua franca of the pub, pupil, press and parliament. The French speak French, the Italians Italian, the Spanish speak Spanish, but unfortunately for the gaeilgeoir mafia, the tongue bequeathed to us by our colonial masters still holds sway. Gaelic is the Irish dichotomy... most people have a guilt about not speaking it but are more than comfortable with the alternative. Maybe, for a nation of storytellers, English, with its malleability, nuances and subtleties of meaning, fell upon the Irish tongue like a tailor-made suit.

Even the "troubadours of the troubles", Ireland's premier folk balladeers, the Wolfe Tones, with a mostly republican repertoire, spent their entire careers lamenting Ireland's woes and lambasting 'perfidious Albion'… in English!

Herewith, a list of master craftsmen whose tool of trade, written, spoken or sung, was the language of the oppressors… Jonathan Swift, Thomas Moore, Edmund Burke, Daniel O'Connell, Charles Stuart Parnell, Oscar Wilde, Sean O'Casey, Brendan Behan, W.B. Yeats, Patrick Kavanagh and latterly Seamus Heaney.

Therefore, as educationalist zealots in Dublin's civil service were endeavouring to get the Irish speaking tail to wag the English speaking dog, this obsession with Gaelic became a daunting task for those moving into secondary school. Failure to pass Irish in the Leaving Certificate was to fail the complete examination. Considering that most of my generation were destined for emigrant ships, this edict was as bizarre as it was ludicrous.

So national school was a lay interlude between the convent habit and the biretta and breviary of secondary school.

The Largy National School was situated on the gradient at the summit of Church Hill, fronting lower O'Neill Park, next to the football ground and within decibel earshot of the Angelus bell.

Largy National School – The "three Rs" by four masters

The four teachers, all married with families of their own, were much more tolerant and sympathetic to the varying abilities of those seated in front of them. Left-handedness no longer seemed like a sinister trait which preoccupied the sisters of St Louis. Each teacher with their own individual teaching methods but still imparting great knowledge.

Master "Dan" Maguire took the first-year reception class for scholars escaping the clutches of the cloisters. Clones born, he taught more or less as trained in St Patrick's College, Drumcondra, in Dublin... by the book, practical, rigid and without flair. He maintained concentration by having us stand for most of the day, lined up along a chalk line edging the classroom.

Master "Paddy" Kennedy taught us almost like an absent-minded professor where daily lessons were a bit chaotic and lacking a thread of continuity. At music lessons, with his singing hopelessly out of key, we reprised the songs of our glorious revolutions. His false teeth, ill-fitting, chatted endlessly in his mouth. But for me, Master Kennedy's class was a breeze, almost a free pass. This was because he and my father were kindred spirits abroad... both Kerry men. Weekly, I was entrusted to bring home for my father's perusal *The Kerryman* newspaper with all its parish pump news and gossip, which my father devoured from cover to cover.

Master "Eoin" McCague from County Tyrone was a native language zealot. Therefore, most of our daily lessons were conducted through Irish and this was the nearest I probably came to being fluent. Flamboyant and expressive, our daily chores were a mixture of drudgery and drama. We re-enacted the Tudor eras by jousting piggyback with rulers as our weapons. We were called up individually to recite chunks of poetry and prose in front of our peers. For instance, Robert Emmet's speech from the dock and Patrick Pearse's oration at the graveside of O'Donovan Rossa.

Our daily maths lesson was an itemised shopping basket and total bill, as follows:

6 oranges @ 1 ½ pence each
2 loaves @ 9 pence each
2 lbs of sausages @ 8 pence each
1 lb bacon rashers @ 10 pence each

A chronic diabetic, Master McCague was prone to flying suddenly into uncontrollable rages for the simplest misdemeanors. We pupils foresaw the impending warning signs... a pallid face, bulging eyes and a quivering jaw. Knowing what was to come, we stood to silent attention by our desks and were individually berated and humiliated in the following manner… "Galvin! I was talking to your father down the town the other day, and he inquired as to how you were doing… I told him you were doing nothing! Absolutely nothing!" This was double-edged, as I faced the wrath of my father as well.

Master "Joe" Kirke, quite fittingly, was the headmaster, and in charge of the ultimate class before third tier beckoned. Easygoing with a laid-back style, ironically, this minimum discipline made us more attentive. He was a heavy smoker with fingers stained by nicotine and had an inner tension which was never facially expressed. A chronic sufferer of psoriasis, he scratched his elbows endlessly through leather-patched sleeves, resulting in flurries of flaky skin trailing in his wake.

But for the poorest of pupils with the brightest of brains, Joe Kirke offered an early step change to their educational potential. By targeting their academic capabilities and with extracurricular studies, most would gain a free scholarship to the prodigious St Macartan's seminary in Monaghan town, itself a gateway to university. For those with musical aptitude, he would offer an alternative career path as a competent saxophonist. Joe Kirke also taught the most musical notation on the most basic instrument… the tin whistle. Those who became accomplished in jigs, reels and hornpipes would diversify to the saxophone, clarinet, trombone and trumpet, joining the myriad of dance bands and showbands of the burgeoning dance hall era.

As headmaster, Master Kirke would subscribe to a bimonthly in-house magazine for all national school teachers nationwide, published by the Irish National Teachers Organisation (INTO). One of its most erudite contributors was the essayist John D. Sheridan. As part of our English comprehension, each scholar in turn faced his classmates to read aloud Sheridan's elegant prose and subtle humour. This would instill in me a lifelong infatuation with the tongue of Shakespeare.

For those of us boys who were either fleet of foot or possessed a bicycle, an extra daily task involved fetching his "repas de midi" prepared by Mrs Kirke at the other end of the town. Just after the Angelus bell, one of us was despatched post-haste, pounding the pavement or pedaling furiously to deliver the midday fare of a sandwich, slice of cake, piece of fruit and piping hot tea, corked in a long-necked bottle, the contents laid in a wicker basket and draped in a tea towel.

As layer after layer of nicotine from John Player untipped cigarettes clung to his lungs, the daily drudge for Joe Kirke from Whitehall Street, across the Diamond, down Fermanagh Street and the challenge of Church Hill became a breathless challenge. The solution for him came in a timely fashion, being one of the first in the town to purchase the now vintage two-stroke moped, the German-manufactured NSU Quickly, which, together with the Volkswagen Beetle, was flooding the Irish market. This sturdy little machine, cheap to buy, became the runaround two-wheeler of choice for teachers, postmen and railway workers alike. Thus, finally, Master Kirke could collect his own dinner.

For the sons of those in dire poverty, their midday rations were literally the breadline and set them apart socially, almost like a Star of David badge. Banished to a small, bleak, cold corrugated shed adjoining the Largy School, they "feasted" on thick slices of bread with margarine and, if lucky, homemade jams washed down with mugs of tea or cocoa. Most of these paupers would take the emigrant ship and, driven with a sense of purpose, carve out successful careers in business and industry.

Secondary School

Departing the easygoing skills of Master Kirke, we now arrived at the educational fork in the road… sitting the primary examination, the Irish equivalent of the "11+". For those who failed, the local technical school offered apprenticeships in manual trades for the boys and bookkeeping for the girls. For those of us who passed, to the gloating joy of our parents, we headed to secondary school. With this generation of mums and dads with basic learning, academic success at secondary level and the possibility of university was the be all and end all. Mothers gossiped across hedgerows and garden gates about future secure careers for their offspring in teaching, local government and the civil service. Two neighbouring guards' wives in the swanky 18 row of O'Neill Park were so obsessed with all things collegiate, Mrs Corrigan and Mrs Lennon were aptly nicknamed "Oxford and Cambridge". Gazing out over the sweep of the town below, arms akimbo, their conversations were peppered with such terms as swatting, studies, revision, cramming and scholarships, passed grades and honour grades, perspiration and inspiration, and certificates.

St Tiernach's Secondary School was situated about a quarter of a mile from the town centre, across the railway gates and on the road to the Fermanagh village of Rosslea. Both school premises and the detached priest residence faced the town's main cemetery, where the frequent corteges of coffins carried shoulder-high was an early reminder of mortality. College for day pupils only, it was an annexe of St Macartan's seminary in Monaghan town, where boarding fees were beyond the reach of most. As I now recollect, my father's annual school fees for both me and my brother was a bargain basement deal at £10 a year.

St Tiernach's Secondary School – Education for Emigration

St Tiernach's School was basic and functional. Sparse of furnishings, classrooms and corridors reverberated daily to the echoing clammer of pimply faces, duck down beards and breaking vocal cords... the rising sap of puberty. Although not as salubrious as the high-flying colleges nationwide... e.g., St Coleman's in Newry, St Mel's in Longford, St Jarlath's in Galway or St Columbkille's in

Derry, nevertheless we traipsed through our humble portals each day to study the exact same curriculum to be tutored by four bachelors in black to no lesser standards.

The head teacher, Father "Packie" Mulligan from Fermanagh, was involved mostly with the school administration. Occasionally, he would take classes to cover absent colleagues. A hardy son of the soil, Father Mulligan was a man of contradictions. A Latin and Greek scholar with a love of classical music, his manner was at once uncouth and refined. Aggrieved or slighted, he would return to the Fermanagh farming block from which he was hewn, becoming gruff, abrupt and abrasive. Alternatively, he set himself the impossible task of imbuing us pupils with an appreciation for classical music.

While we only had ears for rock 'n' rollers, Fr Mulligan would carry his wind-up gramophone and place it carefully on the classroom table. He would then lovingly slide a 78rpm record from its brown dust cover and place it on a wobbly turntable. Dropping on the "stylus", the opening strains of Beethoven's Symphony No. 6 (the Pastoral) hissed through the air as all the while we doodled on our copy books or stared vacantly in the near distance. At various intervals, we would be jolted from our torpor to differentiate between the various instruments. "What's playing now, Galvin?" "It sounds like a flute, Father." "Well, it's an oboe," he replied and, for our knowledge, sketched the various instruments on the chalkboard. We were guided through overtures, arias and intermezzos. We were also amazed to be told that Mozart was only 20 years older than us when he died. Asked to tell the difference between a violin, a viola or a cello, one scholar retorted in typical Clones fashion… "Well, you can't play the big ones under your chin!"

To cope with the sturm and drang of overseeing raucous and over-energised pupils, Packie Mulligan sought solace in the "fishin' 'n' shootin'". He was a master of the rod and reel, fly and float rowlocks and oars on still lakes or wading in weirs. Packie Mulligan was also acknowledged as Ireland's foremost authority on the breeding and training of the Irish Red Setter gun dog. These wonderful dogs with a glossy coat of russet copper, floppy ears and flowing tail gave off the impression of a puppy scatterbrain, such was their sensitivity to the slightest scent or sound. The Setters were so called because of their ability to freeze in half motion at the first scent of ground-nesting game.

Responding thereafter to high-pitched whistle commands, the dog slowly crawled towards its prey, affording the shooter ample time to load and aim. During my tenure at St Tiernach's, Fr Mulligan's working dog, household pet and constant companion answered to the name of Finn, the mythological leader of Celtic warriors, and was addressed in Gaelic only.

On the occasional August evening, Fr Mulligan would beckon me through the open window of his Volkswagen Beetle and address me as such... "Go and tell your mother you're coming hunting with me." With his faithful dog stalking the back seat, we drove over the unapproved border crossing at Lackey Bridge through the hamlet of Aghadrumsee and climbed the long, winding gradient to the high bog moor stretching between Monaghan and Tyrone. With Finn now off the leash, in the rarified air, we followed at some distance through sways of yellow and purple heather, my flimsy canvas gutties sinking in the soft moss and lichen of the high scrubland. As the disturbed wild fowl took flight in the still evening air, my tutorial pastor, he of the pastoral symphony, shotgun locked and loaded, aimed and triggered at their exact trajectory, the birds tumbling to Earth in a barrage of lead shot.

Fr Mulligan, at once gruff, cultured and bookish, never strayed far away from his Fermanagh roots but had a Clones cutting edge. He would end his career in holy orders as the Bishop of Clogher, residing in Monaghan town. With his newly acquired mitre and crozier, he traversed the dioceses, administering confirmation and running a compliant Catholic education system for a compliant Catholic government. He also admonished and absolved miscreants whose cardinal sins only he could forgive... these sins, "quelle horreur!", were the acts of perjury or the illegal drinking of poteen, known as reserved sins, for which my father was one to exclaim sardonically... "As if there weren't enough sins already!"

Father Gallagher came from the ocean's edge of the diocese and my mother's hometown of Bundoran. After his ordination in the early 1950s, he departed Ireland shores to take up a unique sabbatical as a chaplain on a US air force base in California. Returning, Paddy Gallagher had morphed into an all-American guy... "With a dog collar", hence his very apt nickname, the Cisco Kid. When he returned home, he brought with him the fast pace and brashness Americans were known for. His daily discourse was peppered with… "you gotta", "you gonna", "gimme" and "Goddamnit". We pupils were addressed as "you guys", and everything was high octane.

His Sunday morning masses in the local Sacred Heart Church were standing room only for their speed and brevity. As was in the old Tridentine Mass, turning to face the congregation to recite the dominus vobiscum, the manoeuvre was neatly executed by a 360-degree pirouette.

As our history teacher, his knowledge was encyclopaedic. His style was detailed and effusive, referencing neither books nor notes. At the blackboard, his chalk glided on spirit level lines with a unique writing style of Celtic script. His teaching subject was also his abiding hobby and interest, specialising in becoming the country's leading expert on one of the saddest episodes of Anglo-Irish history… the Penal times.

At the latter end of the 17th century, with the reformed church now firmly embedded, the English set about abolishing Catholicism from the face of Ireland. Introducing draconian laws, religious worship was banned, and churches closed or demolished. All Catholics were disbarred from public service, owning property, even a horse. Priests were outlawed, either hunted down or killed, but as with before and after, the more the English imposed, the greater the native resistance. Young seminarians departed for their religious colleges of Toledo, Salamanca and Rome. Returning as priests, they tended their furtive flocks, travelling the countryside masquerading as roving musicians. Masses were arranged and celebrated in dense rural areas, where the altars consisted of large flat stones, known as mass rocks. They are still to be found dotted around the countryside and revered as symbols of defiance. Spending every available spare moment scrubbing moss-covered and broken headstones in ancient graveyards, the Cisco Kid, with his lectures, books and pamphlets, concentrated on an era where the Catholic Church and Irish nationalism would merge as a single force of rebellion.

Asked once to address a party of visiting American tourists in the Great Northern Hotel in Bundoran, he regaled the assembled guests with a two-hour "tour de force" on Irish history with his only "aide-mémoire" being three or four stand-out dates of history scribbled on the back of a cigarette pack. His discourse began with pagan Ireland of the druids, to St Patrick, monastic Ireland, and the rekindling of European culture and learning after the Dark Ages. Hardly pausing for breath, he led his enraptured audience through the Viking invasion, the battle of Clontarf, Norman Ireland, Plantagenet and Tudor rule, Henry VIII and the Reformation, Elizabethan Armada and the false dawn of the Stuart kings. He then continued with the tyranny of Cromwell, Hanoverian restoration, peasant rebellions in the wake of the "sans-culotte", Daniel O'Connell and Catholic freedom, potato blight, starvation and emigration. He followed with Charles Stuart Parnell and agrarian reform, the Fenians, the Easter Rebellion and finally partial independence.

Walking with a pounding footfall and a swaggering cassock and almost tripping over his bandy legs, an isolated tuft of hair fell across his furrowed forehead, which he nervously swept back. The Cisco Kid's intellectual capacity could be best described by the poet Oliver Goldsmith's description of the school teacher in his epic saga "The Deserted Village"

"And still they gazed and still the wonder grew,
That one small head could carry all he knew."

Father "Spud" Murphy taught the subject of my worst nightmares… maths. These hour-long classes filled me with dread and foreboding. Fractions, equations, algebra and geometry turned me into a nervous wreck. His prophecy of my maths markings in my Leaving Certificate Examination was spot on… "Galvin, if it's a nice summer day and the examiner is in a good mood, you'll get just about 40 per cent" (the minimum requirement for a pass). The son of a local engine driver, Fr Murphy was an unabashed social climber and a sadistic bully. A bully in the sense that through corporal punishment, he could turn a maths dunce like me into a budding Einstein. In Fr Murphy's classes, mesmerised by fractions, equations and decimals, I trembled at trigonometry while triangles and rectangles rendered me into an innumerate fool. His carrot and stick approach was stick only and consisted of the most pliable bamboo cane. The alternative favourite was a length of Bunsen burner tubing from the science lab which, by wrapping itself around the outstretched hand, provided a double dose of "encouragement".

A lover of Spain and a fluent speaker, Éamon Murphy spent each of the school summer holidays as a curate in some Galician or Andalusian village where I fervently hoped he would remain. The first person in Clones to own a Volkswagen Beetle, he could have set a national trend. This German car, in regulation black with its low maintenance, air cooled and fuel efficient, became the clerical car of choice throughout the land. It was both spacious enough for an altar boy or a parochial housekeeper in the front. The rear seat became the sole preserve of Irish priestly sport… a set of golf clubs.

For a curate or a parish priest dwelling alone in cavernous houses, the clubs were their doorway to both social climbing and social ingratiation. Still an elite sport, golf offered opportunities to mingle with the movers and shakers of the town. Here, bogged down on tees, fairways, bunkers, greens, eagles, birdies, putters and irons, he mingled with the doctors, dentists, drapers, publicans, grocers and butchers who lived detached lives behind recessed high railings on the periphery of the town.

Father McNaboe was our English teacher and the most inspirational of all. His classes were an oasis of calm, wedged between high-octane history and intimidating maths. He was a native of Dromore, a Tyrone village on the cusp of Clogher Diocese which snaked its way through Monaghan, Fermanagh and South Donegal. Strikingly handsome with black wavy hair, a swarthy complexion and wine-coloured eyes, this holiday matinee idol lookalike was christened Nick Romano. Many townswomen, pillars of the church and with pupils in his care, swooned in his presence or flirted unabashedly full in the knowledge of him being a forbidden fruit. As some would whisper behind cupped hands, "What a waste to the cloth."

The five-year curriculum in our lowly classrooms was as comprehensive as any in the country's leading public schools. It included two Shakespearean plays (in my case, *The Merchant of Venice* and *Hamlet*) and the English poets Keats, Shelley, Coleridge and Wordsworth. For honours grade, we studied the literature of Dickens, Chaucer or Milton. Also included were the Irish poets Thomas Moore, Oliver Goldsmith, W.B. Yeats and James Joyce.

In Sean McNaboe, we had a master tutor who made the imparting of knowledge subliminally simple. A stickler for grammar and pronunciation, his constant mantra was ever thus: "If the greatest colonial legacy is the English language, we should at least speak it properly." A hands-up request of "Please, Father, can I go to the toilet?" was answered with "You can but may not." 'I's were placed before 'E's except after 'C's, and there were definitely no split infinitives in Nick Romano's presence. Reciting large chunks of prose aloud in front of our peers instilled the importance of punctuation in sentence structure. This descendant of a hedge school master in a cassock and from "Tyrone among the bushes" guided us through Shakespeare's iambic pentameter, sonnets, plots and plays... Shylock's woes on the Rialto Bridge, Julius Caesar's duplicitous backstabber Brutus, Cassius and his fickle wife Calpurnia and Hamlet's inner torment at Elsinore.

His bête noire, almost undertaking as a one-man crusade, was to rectify the inability of most Irish to stick their tongue between their teeth and pronounce "th". To his constant frustration and annoyance, "de déficit infliction" prevailed throughout the nation and every social stratum from "de" semi-literate to "de" so-called erudite. Diss (this), dat (that), dese (these) and dose (those) was embellished by "how are tings", as well as mudder (mother), fadder (father) and brudder (brother). At the mere mention of "de udder" (the other), McNaboe, eyes raised heavenward with exasperation, would exclaim... "Udders are for cow byres."

One of the most glaring offenders of de déficit was Bertie Ahern, a former prime minister during the Celtic Tiger years. During his tenure, I do recall an intergovernmental visit to Sweden. At the resulting press conference, the host prime minister spoke perfect English, while "de nort side Taoiseach", with a stumbling syntax and appalling elocution, was a national embarrassment.

Each autumn, Clones locals waited avidly for McNaboe's annual school play production. Out of the cloth, Sean McNaboe could have carved out a stellar career in the field of dramatic art. All the plays he selected were comedies and hilarious. Some were set in Dublin's tenements, others in rural Ireland. Dublin dramas had all the black humour of poverty, farmland dramas were set in thatched cottages with feuding families fighting over legacies and land.

CLONES THE TOWN

The second town in the county, Clones was slung hammock style between two hills. The main street, Fermanagh Street, rose to an elevated square known as the Diamond. In the other direction, the railway crossing bisecting the town would emphasis its importance as the main employer.

The Diamond and Protestant Church

At its pinnacle, the Diamond was dominated by the Protestant church with a dwindling congregation, now almost a mausoleum. Below, the various imposing banks, the police station, the town hall and the library. From here, the three main roads running southward sloped away, connecting the rest of the country, almost like umbilical cords.

Once a British garrison town, some street names still recalled past colonial connections. For instance, Whitehall Street was named after London's seat of power while Jubilee Road reflected Queen Victoria's longevity on the throne. In a flurry of nationalistic fervour post-independence, Whitehall Street was renamed McCurtain Street after the mayor of Cork who died in a hunger strike in Brixton Jail. Jubilee Road was now named '98 Avenue, recalling the brave but doomed

Wexford Rebellion of 1798. Erne Square fronting the station was renamed O'Duffy Square, immortalising a son of Monaghan, Eoin O'Duffy, participant in the fight for freedom who would later gain both fame and infamy. The founder of the Irish police force, The Civic Guards, he would later become a patriotic pariah for raising and leading an Irish brigade to fight on the side of Franco in the Spanish Civil War. Suffice it to say that despite this attempted airbrushing, all three streets were still called by their original names.

An ancient Celtic settlement, Clones still retained relics of its ancient Christian past with monastic ruins, a round tower and a weathered high cross, elevated high on the Diamond.

Fermanagh Street was the usual mix of shops… butchers, bakers, barbers, drapers, footwear, jewellery, confectionery and hardware, builders merchants, chemists and hairdressers. The town also had a plethora of pubs catering for a sizeable cross-border trade where licensing laws were more draconian.

Whitehall Street – AKA McCurtain Street

THE RAILWAY

If the hilltop churches and the evangelical halls were Clones' spiritual, at its material heartbeat was the railway. Bisecting the town, it was the town's main employer and, as such, the "engine" of the local economy. Clones Railway Station, the main junction between north and south, could be described as a mini Clapham Junction, with four platforms, waiting room, dining rooms, a goods yard, turntable and major engineering works.

Employing across the religious divide, it gave the town a buzz of industry. The smells and sounds hung in a pervading pall in the Clones air, the pungent aroma of steam, smoke, grease and oil was added to in summer with vapoured creosote from cured railway sleepers. The town echoed daily to the hissing of steam, juddering shunting wheels and metallic hammering from the cavernous workshops.

At a level crossing, a twinkling lamp and a tinkling bell warned of impending closure. In the junction box nearby, a large ship wheel swung the gates open and closed while a large array of shiny levers controlled the points and signals. In the subway by the railway gates, Jeyes Fluid was spread liberally to counteract the smell of stale urine, as pub patrons nightly emptied their bladders before their staggering ascent of Church Hill and O'Neill Park. In the quiet of the evening, we boys added to the rancid odours standing on the topmost step and arching our urine parabola style to see who could pee the farthest and reach the lowest step.

As a band of brothers, Clones rail workers were a tight knit community in an already close knit local one, as witnessed on pay days, assembling in the nearest hostelry, The Hibernian Hotel AKA "the Tommon". Here, porters, shunters, guards and maintenance men intermingled at the bar behind copious amounts of Guinness with Jameson chasers, while at either end of the town, anxious wives fretted about enough residual wages to settle shopping bills.

Even though the era of steam was reaching its nadir, a summer special excursion on the Bundoran Express, with its liveried carriages hand built in Derby and Swindon, still proved very popular. Departing Dublin daily, its gleaming engine pulling carriages packed to capacity with raucous holiday makers seated on lush and comfortable seats, the train rocked gently along the permanent way. On board, train doors clicked shut with ease and the windows were adjustable by leather straps. Below the luggage racks were framed sepia photographs of Ireland's beauty spots... the Lakes of Killarney, Connemara, the Wicklow Hills and the Mountains of Mourne. With only two stops on the way, the Bundoran Express glided through the railway gates of Clones on the stroke of noon, before its penultimate halt at the station of Pettigo where pilgrims alighted for the penitential island of Lough Derg then onward to the "Queen of Donegal" - Bundoran.

The Great Northern Railway was a generous employer and its employees, misguided by their loyalty and devotion, classified themselves as shareholders. Much to the chagrin of the G.N.R., workers assumed property rights to the company's goods and chattels. As well as the Monaghan stoop, the Clones rail workers perfected the lateral lift as they carried large blocks of coal underarm homewards.

In the railway sidings, stockpiles of shiny black coal, mined from the bowels of Yorkshire, Nottinghamshire, Derbyshire and the Welsh Valleys, were laid out in mini pyramids and were viewed as a perk of the job. This fuel, instead of producing flickering pressure gauges in locomotive cabs, was now keeping winter cottages snug and warm. Neighbours of one employee awoke one morning surprised to see his cottage surrounded by a low whitewashed wall... in reality, interlocking blocks of coal hastily painted overnight. By the end of the following spring, the temporary edifice had literally gone up in smoke. In every Irish Catholic household, a petite Sacred Heart lamp with a blood red dome and resting on a plinth before a picture of the Sacred Heart burned perpetually and held pride of place; the fuel capacity of the burning wick could be measured in teaspoons. So it was with some incredulity, one worker approached the store manager requesting "a wee drop of paraffin for the Sacred Heart lamp" and holding a 10-gallon drum. Others around the town dined on place settings of fine bone china and drank tea from delicate gold-rimmed cups and saucers. Silver service cutlery from Sheffield all bore the provenance logo G.N.R.

As car ownership increased and rail travel decreased, economics were forcing the network "off the rails". The viability of Clones station was inevitably looming. In the last-ditch attempt to stave off the inevitable, a delegation of the town's great and good travelled to Dublin to lobby the relevant government minister. Ushered into his office and seated at his desk, they stated their case for a reprieve with enthusiasm and conviction. The minister, having listened to their heartfelt plea and, in the ensuing silence, pressing his fingers together and staring intently at the petitioners, enquired, "By the way, ladies and gentlemen, how did you travel to Dublin today?" ... "By car" came the unanimous reply. "In that case," he replied, "I rest my case and wish you a pleasant journey home."

"A Ridge of Low Pressure"

Irish weather could only be described as a "tropical rainforest"... without the tropics. The climate would figure largely in local life. Monaghan, with its peculiar topography of rolling hills and water features, both flowing and static, was a weather system within a weather system. Lovingly described by my father as "the pisspot of Ireland", precipitation came in every guise. Winter rains were angled wind-driven shafts of cold steel bouncing off shivering Celtic faces. With the warming days of spring came intermittent balmy "April showers" under arcing rainbows. Evaporating sodden bogs, fields, hedges and woodlands gave rise to the horizontal micro fog, known as "Irish mist". This fog, suspended like a curtain, swirled dank and dense and penetrated everything. Trees stood damp and glistening while telegraph wires swayed with beaded droplets.

High pressure in Clones effected not only the residents' cardiovascular systems but also car tyres. The daily dawn chorus was drowned out by misfiring car engines and flattening batteries. The most efficient Bosch spark plug or Champion contact breaker set were no match for Clones' misty morning air. Flooded carburetors spluttered into life by means of an arm wrenching crank handle or by the clutch, second gear and the nearest available hill. Willing neighbours pushing a stubborn car, rendered the dawn air a mixture of steamy breaths and pungent petrol fumes.

This near constant humidity entered every pore and fibre, taking its toll health-wise. Infirmities were mainly twofold, pulmonary and orthopaedic. Wheezing lungs gasped through nose and mouth with rheumatics, bronchitis, lumbago accompanied by creaking joints, stiffened limbs and stooped frames. As the priest gave his Sunday homily from the pulpit, he would struggle to be heard over a chorus of rattling coughs, clearing throats and muffled sneezing. The only mobility aid of the time was the humble walking stick, whether the gnarled varnished Blackthorn or the bendable yet dependable bamboo.

Because of its unique weather, the town had its very own meteorological station. Perched high above O'Neill Park, its hourly observations were transmitted to the Dublin headquarters. One of its measuring instruments, basic but ingenious, tracked the daily trajectory of the sun. A narrow strip of white cardboard was curved behind a magnifying crystal ball whose intensified rays burned a charred line along its length. Needless to say, on most days of the Clones calendar, it remained scorch free.

And yet, a fleeting glory, when after a day of incessant downpour, the evening sky would clear to a deep azure blue. The warming twilight rays of the setting sun evaporated drying grassland to give off an overpowering aroma and the eerie spectre of low, knee-high fog hanging static over bogs and rushy meadows.

CLONES THE PEOPLE

Almost completely encircled and now a peninsula stretching into County Fermanagh, the locals now abandoned in Ulster and neglected by Dublin (except at elections!) would become resourceful, self-reliant and turn the border to their advantage.

Although mostly Catholic, Clones still contained a sizeable Protestant minority whose businesses were still patronised by all out of a grudging respect for not jumping ship at partition.

Now left in limbo and cut off from their provincial hinterland, townsfolk, by a combination of doggedness and bloody mindedness, turned into "super cute hoors". Everyday discourse was one of sarcasm and cynicism; local wit was sharp and sardonic. Nicknames mirrored both physical and mental frailty, the greater the affliction, the greater the opprobrium.

With its hilly terrain, daily life was a constant battle with gravity and the normal perpendicular gait would evolve into the Clones stoop, where people would promenade one or two degrees forward of the vertical.

Postscript: Schadenfreude

Schadenfreude wouldn't have figured a lot in the Clones vocabulary or tripped off Clones tongues, but unknowingly a certain group of characters turned its practice into an art form. Unencumbered by the distraction of having to do a day's work, and weather permitting, Messrs Frank Nolan, Rinty Monahan and Maurice Reilly pitched up daily at Connolly's Corner, the main junction of the town's streets with a commanding view of all the comings and goings.

Frank, the Prussian, was so called because of his dark, foreboding facial features. His countenance, swarthy and unsmiling, was set in stone as rigid as the US presidents carved into Mount Rushmore. Standing in the classic Clones stoop, hands clasped firmly behind his back, he wore a peak cap pulled down to just above eye level that afforded him the ability of appearing to look straight ahead while performing a 180-degree periscopic sweep. An untipped cigarette, spittle stained to half its length, rested between protruding lips. Once lit, it was never removed. With the burning ash arcing with gravity, Frank, from their Connolly's Corner vantage point, would give a running commentary on all the passers-by with both Rinty and Maurice adding snippets of wisdom.

Fermanagh Street and Connolly's Corner

Vilification was the order of the day, and no one was spared their venom. Physical and mental disorders were grist to the mill. Family histories of one and all were forensically dissected, skeletons rattled and tumbled from cupboards and woe betide returning emigrants displaying any outward signs of newfound wealth. Young able-bodied lads returning from England's building sites with shiny shoes, snazzy suits, slick hairdos and fat wallets were mercilessly lambasted: "Would you look at him with his airs and graces! I well remember the day he left with the arse hanging out his trousers."

Young girls returning from London or New York with stylish makeup, dangling bangles and earrings and the latest fashions were similarly lambasted: "Would you look at her! When she left, she was wearing her sister's hand-me-downs and didn't have a change of knickers!"

CHARACTERS

Barney Reilly

It wasn't that Barney Reilly was work-shy; it was just that the notion of hiring out your energy in a short life for a pittance to enrich others seemed ridiculous. Another reason for Barney's aversion to daily toil was a bucket-list ambition to read the complete contents of Clones Library.

Barney resided with his sister, the breadwinner, on Legar Terrace, an elevated row of artisan cottages hanging precariously between the Rosslea Road below and the Catholic Church above. Apart from the tolling of bells and the shunting of trains in the railway goods yard, Legar Terrace was an oasis of tranquility.

With a rosy elfin face, smooth, shiny and unwrinkled, Barney also sported a mop of sleek black shiny ringlets. During any week, his energy levels were slightly strained as, burdened by an armful of hardbacks lovingly cradled concertina style, he made his way to and from Clones bibliothèque. His metabolism would now revert to torpor as seated in the small front parlour with a turf fire and a ticking clock, Barney lovingly absorbed the pages of history, geography, biography, science, religion, et al. This must have surely been the earliest definition of long-term unemployed... however, with one seasonal exception, the same thumb and index finger which straightened dog-eared pages now went into a frenzy of frenetic activity in the proceeding weeks before Christmas... plucking turkeys. Seated on an upturned egg box at Thompson's Poultry and Egg Store, this polymath plucker compressed one year's work into four weeks. Working at breakneck speed and up to his knees in feathers and quills and a haze of turkey down, Barney could strip the largest cock bird featherless from neck to parson's nose literally in minutes. For decorative purposes, birds were left with a small residue of plumage; the neck and drumsticks were ringed with a small feather collar while the parson's nose was draped over with a fringe of quills.

Having shoehorned so much energy into such a small timespan, his labours ensuring a golden centerpiece on every Christmas table, Barney would wind down again to his natural aversion to "earning his bread by the sweat of his brow" and return once more to the fusty and literary treasure trove that was Clones Library. Barney's reading taste varied with the seasons; weighty tomes with weightier subjects were for long wintery nights in the glow of a paraffin lamp, punctuated by the ticking wall clock, the Angelus bell and the chirruping of crickets behind the hearth. Speed reading novels, romance, light fiction and nonfiction were for summery days and long evenings seated in a súgán chair outside his front door.

Chatting once with his next-door neighbour who was preparing his rear garden for spring sowing and planting, Barney, with his phobia and dread of gardening implements, explained, "Be Jaysus, if any of these were about the house, I wouldn't get a daycent night's sleep!"

Johnny McGahey

For the Catholic majority of Clones, the main venue for social events was St Joseph's Hall, situated halfway up Church Hill between the level crossing below and the convent above. It comprised a main hall, with two smaller function rooms to the left and right of the main entrance; accessed by a flight of steep steps, the foyer ran past these annexes to the larger salle de fete. With the stage at one end and a shiny maple floor, its uses were varied. Apart from dancing, both strict tempo and Irish traditional, it doubled as a theatre for local amateur thespians. In the pre-Advent period before Christmas, the local populace engaged in large card playing whist drive with lots of spot prizes on offer, and for the main winners, a bumper seasonal hamper. End of school summers was the setting for intermediate and final third-level examination.

As a cinema, it gained national notoriety in the late 1940s and early 1950s when, by clerical edict, the audience was separated by gender. Before the lights dimmed on grainy black and white cowboy westerns or the comic exploits of Laurel and Hardy or Charlie Chaplin, married couples suffered the indignity of having to sit apart. This moral zone ensured eyes fixed on the screen in the dark and no sins of the flesh took place by wandering hands.

The two front annexes performed different purposes. To the right was a room with two tables, one for the billiard purists and the other for snooker. This room was normally enveloped in a twilight of gloom, save for the twin overhead canopies beaming light on the green baize. This was further dimmed by a fog of cigarette smoke and coal fumes from a large hearth radiating a golden glow. On winter nights, this inferno was encircled by heat-seeking arses, the only audible sounds being of low frequency chatter and the clicking of ivory balls. The opposite room was for social soirées and card playing and, like the best establishment clubs dotted around St James' in London, were male-only enclaves.

It also happened that my teenage years would coincide with the twilight years of combatants of both the Great War and the Irish War of Independence. Seated in the midst of these retirees, we listened spell-bounded to tales of living history. The irony was that while Irish men in British regiments fought on the Western Front to free France and Belgium from German occupation, fellow Irishmen on home soil were fighting to free Ireland from British occupation. Reminiscing soldiers on both sides regaled us children with tales of trench warfare and going over the top in Flanders, their heroic deeds displayed showing their gallantry medals. "The Boys of the Old Brigade" recalled the Easter Rising, the David versus Goliath guerilla War of Independence against "Perfidious Albion" and starting the rot of the British Empire under a new banner... the Irish tricolour. Now in old age, all these Irishmen, their old allegiances now forgotten, the hatchet was well and truly buried.

Overseeing the maintenance of this social hub was the caretaker Johnny McGahey, himself with some distasteful social habits. His first aversion was to change any garment inner or outer. His second aversion was to water, not between cup and lip or boiled in a teapot, but when moistened with a bar of soap. His trousers were shiny and silted with grease and grime from belt to bellbottoms. His waistcoat, once slate grey, was now stained brown with dried saliva. His cloth cap sweat-rimmed and concealing tufts of matted hair was multifunctional, doubling as a handkerchief, coal scuttle, and a billiard table brush. His constant chewing of large chunks of plug tobacco reduced his molars to nicotine-stained stumps, but his jawbone muscles, toned from a million chompings, would ensure an alligator grip. Johnny's pièce de résistance was his mastery of the long-distance spit; disposing of a constant supply of stained saliva carried out with pinpoint crosshair accuracy. Standing at the topmost hall steps in the evening, nuns returning from their school duties below and convent bound were greeted by a deferential doff of his cap and an overhead lob of brackish gob. Once airborne, the expectorant rose in an arc until, succumbing to gravity, it dropped with a splat in the middle of the roadway. On cold winter evenings, where bodies formed a semicircle around the blazing hearth in the billiard room, Johnny, finding the smallest aperture between the huddle, lobbed a mass of liquid nicotine firewards, covering the embers like an extra layer of fuel.

With clogged sweat glands from forehead to feet and clothing starched with the years of grime, local cynics had a field day. Some reckoned Johnny hadn't washed since the midwife gently soaked him down and swaddled him at birth. Another described how on entering Monaghan Hospital for surgery in a pre-procedural bath, a nurse discovered a cotton vest he was unaware he was wearing.

Johnny Mullarkey

Johnny Mullarkey was a local painter and decorator. Somewhat hard of hearing, his eyesight more than compensated, hanging wallpaper with plum line perfection and using master strokes to obtain unblemished paintwork on walls and woodwork.

Up until the DIY boom from the 1970s, paint ingredients, especially gloss, were a lethal mixture of lead, zinc and mercury. Unaware of the long-term effects, painters on a daily basis ingested these fumes, especially in closed spaces, leading to chronic long-term gastro/digestive conditions such as colic, ulcers and kidney and liver failure, and this was reflected in their pallid, bloodless faces. Like all other Clones tradesmen, Johnny was a master of the "suck in sigh". Asking for the most basic quote for a job would elicit a sharp intake of breath through protruding lips, clenched teeth and a sideways nod. The unsuspecting customer would now be hit with more add-ons than a Ryanair ticket. A litany of possible pitfalls and extras would follow… uneven walls, split walls, preparation, putty replacement, blowlamp scraping, sandpapering and priming… the list became endless, and usually prefaced with "well, for a start" "not to mention", "besides" and "then you have".

Johnny's main pastime was as an avid collector of objets d'art. His little artisan cottage at the far end of town was an Aladdin's cave of pictures, pottery, antique books, musical instruments and various treasured family heirlooms. The trouble was, all the acquisitions were gleaned from clients' houses... and without their permission! A kleptomaniac, Johnny was to be observed most evenings going homeward, brushes and paint tins in one hand, and a violin case tucked in the other. As everyone in town was aware of his affliction, most victims would use a simple trick to retrieve their goods temporarily removed. The simple ploy of "borrowing" their items back was very effective: the teacher could reclaim his dictionary, citing homework for scholars. Fiddles, flutes, accordions and banjos would be needed for some up-and-coming musical event. Paintings, wall and mantelpiece ornaments were cajoled back into kitchens, parlours and sideboards.

Johnny "the Jazzer"

Johnny Maguire was unique in a town where a lot of able-bodied men couldn't or wouldn't work. Here was an individual with a major physical impairment, who engaged in quite hard physical employment: a local council employee, his task was to keep trim all the town's roadside verges and hedgerows. The victim of a stroke, and virtually paralysed down one side, he utilised his two basic implements, a billhook and a slash hook, with considerable single-handed skill. Grassy edgings were manicured to tennis court finesse, bushes shaped and clipped, but for all his hard work efforts under severe bodily limitations and working in all weathers, his walking gait would earn him a true Clones nickname, apt, denigrating and cynical. Moving with some difficulty and imbalance, his limited stride transformed into a jaunty hop and skip. This was interpreted as a kind of jitterbug dance move from the "roaring 20s" hence his nickname, "Johnny the Jazzer".

Oh Ye Oh Ye Oh Ye!

Jimmy Crosgrove was a local town crier, nicknamed "Jimmy Cuckoo"; its origins preceded its generation into the mists of time.

One possible explanation is that, perhaps as an only child, this cruel jibe, Clones style, was aimed at parents with one infant, recalling the breeding habit of the cuckoo, a summer visitor from Africa, depositing its single egg to be reared parasitic style in some other bird's nest.

A public servant of Post-Imperial Ireland, Jimmy wore the drab garb of the new Republic, in contrast to the sartorial trappings of his English counterpart who wore a tricorne hat with feathered plumes, velvet braided frock coat with ruffled sleeves, breeches, silk stockings and buckled shoes. Instead, Jimmy's attire could have been plucked from a propaganda poster of a Chairman Mao comrade during "the Long March"... a floppy peaked cap sheltered a hanged down face, mournful eyes and a drooping Mexican moustache. A long faded scarf, cravat style, was tucked inside a threadbare jacket which hung ill-fittingly over stooped shoulders. Standing in the classic Clones style, his upper body rigid, he strode from the knees downward inside baggy trousers and hobnail boots as he pounded the pavements with a brass brown bell. Now, slowed down by age and arthritic joints, Jimmy would pause for breath throughout the town's ups and downs. Leaning against the nearest available prop, he would proclaim hoarsely, "The town water will be turned off at midday and remain turned off until the evening."

Here we mischievous school children peering out by a nearby alleyway would remind him of a depredation from his past. Years before our time, Jimmy Crosgrove is said to have borrowed a hammer from a near neighbour which he has reputed to have never returned. Berating him mercilessly, we followed him from alleyway to alleyway, pied piper style, shouting in unison, "Leave back the hammer!"

The Tennessee Waltz

Joey "the Gamm" Maguire and Johnny "Glitter" Reilly were not only near neighbours, but "brothers in arms". Living doors apart at the apex of O'Neill Park, their labours were a joint endeavour... manufacturing concrete building blocks. Their workplace was the timberyard at the rear of Morgan's hardware and general store, a repetitive and monotonous job they toiled in all weathers. It could be said this partnership would cement their friendship.

Joey worked the block making machine, primitive and manually operated while Johnny knocked up mixture. With years of experience, he could gauge the exact aggregate mixture of sand to cement merely by the turn of his shovel.

The compound was now poured into the machine comprising four rectangular moulds compressed and then ejected. They were then transferred to metal shelving open to the elements and laid out in serried ranks like Chinese terracotta soldiers. Drying out would be completed hopefully by the sporadic sun and breezes emanating from the Gulf of Mexico.

Working out in the elements and inhaling large quantities of sand and cement particles induced a thirst that required some slaking. Having expended vast energy at work, Joey or Johnny didn't do hunting, fishing or gardening as did their wives knit, sew or crochet. Instead, every Saturday evening, suited and booted, and linked by their spouses, they strolled down Church Hill for an evening of alcoholic excess in the town's pubs. The object of this weekly soirée was to get totally hammered, or in Clones parlance, "stocious drunk".

Both men were attired in tweed jackets, summery slacks and polished brogues - Joey with a floppy chapeau cocked at a jaunty angle and Johnny's wire cropped ginger crew cut was Brylcreemed and shiny.

Their merry wives, decked out in snug-fitting jackets, one in yellow and the other in blue with matching blouses and pleated skirts, were coiffed with bouffant perms, large earrings banging and dangling to complement mascaraed eyes, rouged cheeks and cherry red lipstick.

As were the norms in de Valera's Free State, women's role in society was basically threefold, best described in German as Kinder, Küche, Kirche, or best translated into demure English as cooking, catechism and copulating. Pubs then were male-only preserves with women permitted into the purdah "snugs". Snugs were confessional-type alcoves tacked onto the end of bars. Here, served through an almost secret sliding hatch, housewives gossiped sipping fashionable Cinzano and Babychams from schooner glasses, embellished with glazed cherries on cocktail sticks.

However, the brickmakers' spouses, ignoring both convention and condemnation, would shatter the sherry glass ceiling and stood by their men. Standing out in a heaving mass of disapproving looks of disdain and snide comments behind cupped hands, these two "glamour babes" who were breaking the mould and didn't know their place, were already reading their thoughts. These two merry wives of O'Neill Park stared them down and gave as good as they got: "You fuckin' wee runt, if it wasn't for a woman, you wouldn't be here in the first place." Another withering putdown was pure Clones: "To think people have been breeding for millions of years to end up with a cunt like you."

The homeward trek would not be straightforward as they faced the daunting challenges of gravity and balance and Church Hill. Ascending the steep incline, dishevelled and the worse for wear, both men with crumpled jackets, ties undone and lips crusted with congealed Guinness, leaned for support on their ladies, who were equally unkempt with runny mascara and smudged rouge and lipstick. Pausing at the halfway stage of Church Hill by Suzy Clerkin's confectionery emporium, they caught their breath by having a fag. When they approached Sacred Heart Church, the dimly lit streetlights of O'Neill Park beckoned in the gloom before them. Continuing on their journey home, rolling along house front railings for support or shock-absorbing bushes, Joey the Gamm now broke into his weekly rendition of "The Tennessee Waltz":

> I was dancing with my darlin' to the Tennessee waltz
> When an old friend I happen to see
> I introduced him to my loved one
> And while they were dancing
> My friend stole my sweetheart from me

> *Chorus*
> I remember the night of the Tennessee waltz
> I know now just what I have lost
> Yes, I lost my little darlin'
> The night they were playing the beautiful Tennessee waltz

His weekly cabaret audience comprised for the most part sanctimonious women standing in the doorways of lower O'Neill Park taking the high moral ground, tut-tutting with arms folded and eyes rolling. Undaunted, Joey insisted on his weekly encore, slurring the lyrics of "Irene, Goodnight":

40

Last Saturday night I got married
Me and my wife settled down
Now, me and my wife are parted
I'm gonna take another stroll downtown

Chorus

Irene, goodnight
Irene, goodnight
Goodnight, Irene
Goodnight, Irene
I'll see you in my dreams

Sometimes I live in the country
Sometimes I live in town
Sometimes I take a great notion
To jump into the river and drown

Chorus

Stop ramblin', stop your gamblin'
Stop staying out late at night
Go home to your wife and family
Stay there by your fireside, bright

Chorus

Fish 'n' Chips

The proprietors of the town's fish 'n' chip shop would have arrived by a quite circuitous route. Ernesto Scappaticci and his wife Maria, both with broad Belfast brogues, could trace their ancestry back to Southern Italy. In the country of Murphys, McCarthys and O'Flahertys, the surname Scappaticci stood out like a pork pie in Jerusalem. Also, in a populous of fair skin, blue eyes, red hair and freckles, their physical features would set them apart.

The Italians, arriving in the British Isles after the war, brought a new dining experience to the humble spud. The potato, Ireland's staple veg, was enshrined in the Irish psyche in its long and sad history, where the potato famine is etched into every school child's memory. Instead of boiling, mashing or roasting, the Irish were introduced to a "nouvelle cuisine". By cutting spuds into rectangular slices, encasing fish in a flour-based batter and then deep frying both in the main ingredient of the Mediterranean diet, olive oil, they were wrapped and presented in a paper funnel, drenched in vinegar, smothered in salt and doused with ketchup. Thus, a whole new dimension was added to the humble tuber.

The mind indeed boggled as to how the Scappaticci elders departed the heel of Italy for the cold, rainy streets of Belfast. What a culture shock! From the cradle of the Renaissance to the bedrock of bigotry. From the land of Michelangelo, Leonardo da Vinci and Machiavelli to the Orange Lodge of Magheraveely just two miles across the border. From the music of Vivaldi, Rossini and Verdi, to the shrill intimidating fifes and drums of apprentice boy bands marching in triumphant celebration of 300-year-old battles. From the baroque architecture of Rome, Milan, Turin and Venice to the rows of Titanic terracing overlooking Belfast's shipyards.

Ernie Scappaticci was small in stature, squat and stocky in build. Two sad black olive eyes stared out from a waxy sallow face. Above, a mop of raven-coloured thick wavy hair swept backwards from mid-forehead to the nape of his neck and his 5 o'clock shadow was midnight blue. From his lips below a pencil-thin moustache, an untipped John Player cigarette hung nonchalantly. A chain smoker, inhaling every puff long and slow, the nicotine and tar reached the deepest recesses of his, by now, toasted lungs.

Standing almost as broad and long, Ernie was supported by size 12 feet and certainly no pushover. Not only different by name and pigment, but true to his macho Italian roots, Ernesto Scappaticci was a dandy dresser. His sartorial elegance stood out in a frumpy Ireland of ill-fitting jackets and suits in three colours: grey, navy blue and black. For Ernie, glove-fitting, hand-stitched suits in lighter, brighter shades were delivered from bespoke tailors in Dublin or Belfast. Jackets were contoured perfectly on broad shoulders, lapels sloped down to double-breasted buttons. Side pockets were patterned slits and slightly angled, while peeping from his breast pocket, a crisp embroidered linen handkerchief. Trousers with razor-edge seams rested on patent leather or crocodile slip-on shoes, embellished with either buckles or tassels.

Despite all this peacock finery, the chain-smoking Beau Brummell of Fermanagh Street was at once dour, unsmiling and a man of very few words. As a consummate billiard player and with his torso almost in line with the table, his eagle eye could calculate ball positioning without the need to bend down. We schoolboys, seated all around in the smoky shadows, envied Ernie's two prized possessions, his own billiard cue, locked safely in its own case, and his silver cigarette case. This he would slip easily from his inside pocket and, with panache, click open to reveal parallel rows of John Players secured behind elastic bands.

The chip shop itself was in a prime location in mid Main Street and consisted of the shop entrance with four alcoves on either side. Each alcove had seating for six people facing, and in the middle, a Formica table with the requisite condiments. Ernie's wife Maria, who was front of house, peered above two glass display cases, one to keep hot food hot, and the other for chilling soft drinks. A granddaughter of Bari, Napoli or somewhere in between, Maria wore the religious artefacts of Catholic Italy on a gold chain around her neck... the Madonna, a crucifix and Pope Pius XII. On the shelves behind, between cordial bottles, were statues and replicas of various saints. Meanwhile in the kitchen at the rear, Ernie lovingly ladled anaemic potato slices and battered fish into two deep fryers of foaming olive oil. Minutes later, the chips would emerge, dry, crisp and golden brown, together with cod, skate, haddock or sole encased in the thinnest, tastiest batter.

What attracted most of the town's youth at Scappaticci's, like a moth to a candle, was the jukebox standing in one corner. All chrome and flashing lights, we could ape and replay the rock songs in vogue with four plays costing sixpence. The disc of 45rpm, once selected, was retrieved by a rotary arm and laid on a wobbly turntable. On cold, wet, miserable evenings, we huddled around the machine and warmed by the kitchen, clubbed our coppers together as the cafe reverberated to the latest pop songs. However, with the Devil tempting idle minds, on one particular evening, our meagre money dissipated, we hatched a devilish plan to add a "fresh condiment" to the tables. Removing all the vinegar bottles surreptitiously, we retired to an alleyway and emptied the existing contents and refilled the bottles with our very own home brew... the residue of our kidneys. We returned just in time as cinema goers were beginning to queue and jostle at the counter. We looked on with glee as the recycled vinegar, lighter in shade and still lukewarm, was liberally splashed around. We only became alarmed at the repercussions of our dastardly deed when we saw my own sister, who was holding a large cone of chips, reach for the bottle. We tried to warn her but she just shook her head and guffawed in disbelief: "G'way out of that. Sure you're having me on, Jerry."

THE BORDER

In the gerrymandered six counties of northeast Ireland, religious fissures ran deep. These wounds of history were never more raw and exposed than in the observance of the third commandment. For the torch bearers of Martin Luther or the adherence of Henry the VIII's libidinous quest for a male heir, the Sabbath was a day of total inactivity. After Presbyterian and Methodist morning services Wesleyan hymns of Protestant Ulster... Love Divine All Love Excelling, Be Thou My Vision, For Those in Peril on the Sea, Dear Lord and Father of Mankind, and How Great Thou Art wafted heavenward from evangelical halls dotted along the shorelines of Lough Neagh and Lough Erne. Churchgoers then returned to prim parlours with a St James Bible for a day of quiet reading and reflection. Reformation churches in the province were stern places, sparsely furnished save for rigid pews and sermon lectern. Singing worshippers were accompanied by a foot-pumping harmonium. Crucifixes were devoid of any imagery, while braided vestments, incense, Latin liturgy or expansive rituals would be total anathema.

Alternatively, for Catholics, Sunday was a day for revelry. After morning mass, "Roman legions" streamed to festivals, both cultural and sporting. Towns emptied for seaside excursions as all the while pristine Protestant boys and girls trooped to afternoon Sunday schools for more chapter and verse. Catholic children, also in their Sunday best, badgered their elders for a sugary supply of lemonade, lollipops, ice cream and sticks of rock. All this Popish decadence was frowned upon with Cromwellian puritan disdain wherever Union Jacks fluttered. For Catholics, a whole day devoted to scrutinising the old and new testaments was looked upon as killjoy austerity.

All this cauldron of inter-Christian conflict was encompassed by a wayward straggling line which curved and carved its way from the Irish Sea in the east to Lough Swilly in the northwest. County Down in the eastern flank was buffered by County Louth in the province of Leinster. Monaghan, Cavan and Donegal of the "ancien regime" now lined up against the new Ulster of Armagh, Tyrone and Fermanagh. County Leitrim would be the only county in the province of Connacht to toehold a sliver of Fermanagh. At its most northwest extremity, where Donegal faced Derry, the border now became liquid, an imaginary line running through the centre of Lough Foyle. Hereafter, the border would make an acute U-turn and become embedded in every loyalist/unionist mindset.

Drawn up with indecent taste, the British border in Ireland, for its entirety, would wind its way along roadside gullies, beside railway lines, bisecting lakes and rivers and even dividing farms. By merely moving livestock between fields, their national status was altered by the stroke of an ashplant. Known salient, the border could, like spiralled fingers, loop across sections of the same road, both major and minor. This meant cycling, walking or driving across both jurisdictions at short intervals, which my father amusingly referred to as "Fermanagh hopscotch". The brewing of poteen, illegal whiskey, was distilled along its entirety for its ease in jumping across either side undetected. Here also, religious favour and ideology gave way to economic reality. The most loyal of Her Majesty's subjects had few qualms about filling their cars, tractors and lorries with cheaper southern fuel. On the other hand, fervent nationalists who wrapped themselves in the green, white and orange and sang rebel ballads of England's historical wrongs, parked their patriotism and principles in the supermarket car parks of Strabane, Newry, Enniskillen and Omagh for budget buying.

"The Tar in the Road"

My father's workplace, Clones Frontier Post, didn't exactly showcase the newly liberated utopian Ireland. A dark green rudimentary corrugated shed, it stood one mile outside the town and a quarter of a mile from the change of tar in the road. Just outside the town's utilities, working conditions were Dickensian. A Turkish bath in summer, it froze in winter, and air conditioning was provided by wind whistling through open nail holes. Lit nightly by a moth-attracting Tilley lamp, cooking was by a Primus stove whose roar was greater than its firepower. Heating was a turf-fired hearth, ablutions were performed in a dry chemical toilet at the rear, which on summer days gave off malodorous fumes.

Approaching vehicles rolled up to a large wooden barrier bearing the notice "Customs Stop". Drivers would exit their vehicles and proceed through a narrow foyer to a partitioned office window and counter. Here my father would date, stamp and countersign all documentation, always signing his name in Gaelic, a task he estimated he repeated over a million times.

If a regular traveller, my father would engage in local banter about family, friends and weather, often escorting them back to their cars. In the era of pre mass car ownership, daily crossings were intermittent and sporadic. Small surges would occur for Sunday church, Sunday football, fair days and holiday traffic. Border tourists in post-war Ireland were as rare as arctic explorers. Wealthy Britons in their Jaguars and Humbers would arrive, having mistakenly strayed on the wrong road. The occasional German and French with their triptyque passes arrived more out of curiosity, where my father would escort them back to their cars, marking out maps, suggesting scenic routes and trying to fathom out a left-handed steering wheel.

Tall and erect with gleaming shoes, razor-pleated trousers, braided sleeves and cap badge, Assistant Preventive Officer Galvin cut an imposing figure and exuded authority. His fastidious uniform pride was a throwback to his earlier curtailed career as a police officer. Known by all and sundry along the border, my father would always be formally addressed as Mr Galvin. Apart from the intermittent idling of the internal combustion engine, my father's background of easy listening was wraparound and rural, the patter of rain hammering on a tin roof, the wind rustling through cracks, crevices and rusty nail holes, the dawn chorus and the evening offering of the corncrake and cuckoo calling across misty bogs and meadows. Custom posts would close nightly at midnight and any later traffic exiting to the North would have to make a "request" for a nominal fee of two shillings; my father would remain in post to facilitate legal re-entry. Requests were mostly obtained by dance bands playing in cross-border venues. My mother being informed of his change in work shift by a passing motorist, "operation takeaway" would quickly take place: a sandwich of my father's favourite loaf was filled with salad, ham or leftover cold meats together with a triangular slice of either apple pie or sponge cake; which were then placed into a cloth napkin. The accompanying beverage of strong, hot tea, milked and sugared, was decanted into a bottle, cork and screw topped. Ambient temperature was maintained by being placed inside two rolled socks. Placed in a wicker basket, it swayed precariously as one of us children pedalled furiously in the evening air. Here in the gloom, my father dined alone, the turf embers and the light from the suspended Tilley lamp casting eerie shadows.

My father's nightly solitude was frequently broken by the occasional wobbling cyclist or swaying stroller returning from the town's many pubs. One of the regular night owls heading homeward was "Thrupenny bit McDonald". From the townland of Clonmaulin over the border, Pat McDonald was a daily communicant in Clones' pubs. Soft-hatted, tweed-blazered and briar-piped, postmeridian, he would set off at a gentle pace for an afternoon and evening of Guinness and conviviality… courtesy of the British taxpayer. Unemployed or unemployable long term because of blatant sectarian discrimination, Thrupenny bit McDonald confined his work ethic to the bedroom. As with most Catholic broods, he put the "family" into "family allowance". Breeding for benefits ensured a regular income from Her Majesty's treasury. Post-war governments of every hue would be more than dismayed that their social largesse was subsidising cross-border public houses. The irony of all this was that, by denying Catholics equal job opportunities, Protestants with their two-child families were unwittingly changing the population demographics. Arriving at the custom post, slightly unsteady and somewhat the worse for wear, he would offer my father a brace of large Guinness bottles dangling dangerously from jacket pockets. On other nights, two miniature whiskey bottles known as "Baby Powers" would be slid across in my father's direction. Conversation was local, parochial and agricultural... late frosts, early cabbage, potato varieties, livestock, turf cutting and inevitably births, deaths and marriages.

Besides his clerical duties, my father was obligated to do border patrols on his sturdy, high-framed Raleigh bicycle, scouring back roads and side roads for any signs of smuggling activity. This was normally a futile gesture as the smugglers were always one step ahead. More often than not, he would meet up with a colleague from Her Majesty's Customs and Excise at a convenient border crossing for a mutual chat of all things customs.

As well as checking the land barrier, my father was also compelled to patrol people's minds, censorship being alive and well in de Valera's Free State. The Catholic Church would advise the Dublin authorities that certain literature was most unsuitable for innocent Irish eyes. All books and magazines with a sexual content, anti-clerical or communist sentiment was listed and proscribed. The offending list was posted to all customs officials and my father would paste it into his regulations book. If sighted at any border crossing, they were to be seized and destroyed.

Excise regulations also pertained to Clones Railway Station where two officers were permanently assigned. While Officer McInerney was tall, pale, slim and erect, Customs Officer Lynagh was conversely small, squat, rotund and ruddy-cheeked, and both were aptly nicknamed "Mutt and Jeff". Their remit being to check goods wagons shunted into sidings against manifest lists. They could also search passengers in transit. Personal smuggling was confined to food staples with wide price differentials: bacon and sausages were flat packed behind trouser belts, inside knickers or tucked into socks, butter on cold days was concealed under soft hats of female millinery. Messrs McInerney and Lynagh would direct suspicious miscreants to the duty office. There, seated in front of a blazing coal fire, the contraband would slowly ooze clarified down over eyelids and behind glazed ears.

Postscript

For all of his working life, my father trod a very adroit, diplomatic line. Coming from the other end of the country, he never quite came to grips with the internecine war of attrition bubbling below the rivers, lakes, bogs, moors, meadows and mountains of this most picturesque province.

He turned a Nelsonian blind eye to trivial transgressions such as shopping for basic foodstuffs. Protestant farmers along the other side admired him for his non-judgemental attitude, and as a result, our household was inundated with "marshal aid" consisting of fruit, vegetables, meat and poultry. The bog where we cut our turf, owned by a Mr Morton, and a mile into County Fermanagh, was offered at a peppercorn rent.

But the most bizarre token of appreciation was courtesy of British nobility. While on duty one day, a sleek black Rolls Royce pulled up at the roadside barrier. A chauffeur, in full livery, approached to be "stamped in". Inquiring as to who was the passenger of this rare vehicle, the driver informed my father he was chauffeur for the Earl of Caledon, owner of a stately pile in County Tyrone. Engaging the Earl with courteous conversation, my father returned to the office, only to find the car's passbook still lying on the counter. Commandeering the following vehicle to drive at speed, documents and driver were reunited. Thinking no more of it, it was with some surprise returning post-haste to the frontier post, the noble earl praised my father's quick thinking, thanking him in profusion and requested his name, rank and home address. My father thought, perhaps, a letter of commendation might find its way to Customs HQ in Dublin.

However, a week before the following Christmas, the self-same Rolls Royce glided to a halt outside our humble council house in O'Neill Park. As neighbouring curtains twitched, my mother was proffered a large, odd-shaped parcel wrapped in sturdy brown paper and tied in twine, each knot sealed with red wax and bearing the heraldic imprimatur of the Earl of Caledon. Unwrapping it, my mother was presented with a haunch of venison. Leafing through a fusty, faded cookery book for inspiration, she decided on a large casserole. Devoid of the recommended seasoning, garlic being unknown, the deer leg was diced together with chopped carrots and onions. A bouquet garni of Oxo cubes was added, placed in a cast iron pot, and left simmering on a long, low heat. It's ironical that as we dined on the sumptuous fare of kings and queens on our own lowly kitchen table decorated with oil cloth, the accompanying side dish was so basic and so Irish: a pyramid pile of boiled potatoes, with jackets bursting, was laid centre stage. Fork speared, they were peeled, snow-salted and butter-drenched.

DEV

Éamon de Valera was an enigma, wrapped up in a legend, shrouded in controversy. Born in New York to a Galician father and a Limerick mother, his DNA would suggest a fusion of Spanish passion and Irish charm. Au contraire, we find a personality more in mould of the Ulster Scottish Presbyterian, cold, aloof, unsmiling and ascetic. Nevertheless, he bestrode Irish contemporaries of Churchill, De Gaulle, Franco and Salazar.

One of the leaders of the 1916 rebellion, he was spared the executioner's bullet by virtue of his U.S citizenship. Elected president of the first unofficial Dáil, he despatched a delegation including Michael Collins and Arthur Griffiths to London to negotiate a treaty. This motley band of Irish rebels, just off "the run" were no match for the diplomatic skills of the "Welsh Wizard" Lloyd George, Prime Minister of an empire, Winston Churchill and Lord Birkenhead. They returned to Dublin with a fait accompli, ultimatum agreement of a 26-county Free State, Ulster partition dominion status, and an oath of allegiance to the reigning monarch. de Valera was incandescent.

Put to a democratic vote of acceptance by parliament and people, de Valera split with former comrades-in-arms, formed a rebel breakaway rabble group and plunged the country into a vicious internecine civil war. It pitted fathers against daughters, mothers against sons and brothers against sisters, whose legacy defines Irish politics to this very day. Defeated by the forces of the fledgling State "the long fellow" sought purdah in the vineyard of sour grapes vowing never to accept the treaty.

But the "Spanish onion in the Irish stew", having licked his wounds, re-emerged phoenix-like in the late 20s, and formed his own political party, Fianna Fáil. He was elected and accepted the previously unacceptable and bestrode Irish politics for 50 years.

A mathematics teacher who couldn't run an economy, "Dev" was the Marmite of his era. My father loathed him for his division and destruction he caused, and indirectly the assassination of Michael Collins. My auntie Bridie, on the other hand, in lively discussions around the Bundoran kitchen table, revered de Valera almost messiah-like, declaring she would "eat the grass off the side of the road for the man".

His vision of Ireland, a small self-sufficient island marooned off mainland Europe, would be a society rural, agricultural, conservative, Catholic and Gaelic speaking. Its symbol of virginal purity was his modest description of Irish womanhood..."comely maidens dancing at the crossroads".

Dev's economic safety valve for unemployment lay in cross channel ferries and transatlantic steamers. de Valera fiddled while young Ireland roamed and a generation of young Irish men headed for the building sites of London, Manchester and Birmingham to reconstruct post war Britain. Young Irish girls with their natural in built rapport and patient empathy became the nursing mainstay of wards in the fledgling National Health Service.

Others, following in the footsteps of their famine forebears, scraped together the fare and sailed away to the "Land of the Free and Home of the Brave". Police precincts from New York, Chicago, Boston and Los Angeles were patrolled by O'Malleys, O'Sheas and O'Rourkes. This is also where the ebb tides of the ports of Dublin, Rosslare and Cork were replenished with the tears of Irish emigrants.

But whether venerated or vilified, this son of New York via Bruree in County Limerick, this man of rebellious war, War of Independence, Civil War and economic war with Britain, would, by keeping neutral in World War II, afford me and my generation the eternal gratitude of an idyllic childhood.

Cocooned away from the anguish, both mental and physical, of a world at war... Not for us starvation, deprivation and lack of education. Not for us too were battlefield wastelands or aerial bombardments. Most Irish were ambivalent about the conflict raging across Europe. On the one hand, they gloated that the Sassenach were getting a bloody nose. Alternatively, newly independent, they were fearful that their 700-year struggle against the "auld enemy" would be overrun by the Nazi jackboot.

Together with the Swiss and Swedes, we observed this cauldron of conflict from a safe distance fully aware of the repercussions of Hitler's aspirations, but in true Irish style, in a master stroke of understatement, the period from 1939 to 1945 would be known quite simply as "The Emergency".

COLD WAR WARRIORS -
FACING THE RUSSIAN THREAT

At the tender age of 15, I and my classmates enrolled in the Irish Territorial Army. Originally known as the L.D.F. (Local Defense Force), it was renamed the Gaelic equivalent - Forsa Cosanta Aituil (F.C.A.) but sardonically referred to by one and all as the "Free Clothing Association". Joining up three years before the age of legal eligibility, our enthusiasm was more monetary than patriotic

The Quartermaster of the Monaghan Battalion and a Clones resident, Matt Byrne, kitted us out more by eye glance than measuring tape. Our drill hall, a small annexe behind St Joseph's Hall, was where we assembled weekly preparing to repel any foreign invader. Our uniform consisted of beret with rear ribbons, a brass cap badge, a high collared tunic with brass buttons that were embellished with the Irish harp, and trousers which were manufactured from coarse material almost akin to horse hair. Many a military mother made the necessary alterations with needle and thread taking up the tunic sleeves that drooped over hands and the trousers that trailed the floor. The cloth was almost as abrasive as sandpaper, constantly chaffing necks and legs. This "Pret-a-Porter" collage was completed and complimented by a broad brown leather belt, leggings and oversized "divers boots". Double sets of winter wooly socks compensated for adolescent feet slopping around size 9/10 boots.

Our weaponry, to combat the nuclear threat, was a classic antique from the Great War and a job lot purchased from Britannia. The Lee Enfield 303 was far too heavy and cumbersome for our teenage hands and shoulders. During storage, the working parts were kept oiled, which in turn seeped into the woodwork, which in turn oozed onto sleeves and hands on sunny days. Sloping arms which involved transferring the gun from the ground, across the torso to the right shoulder, was for our 15-year-old arms like lifting a sack of spuds.

On summer Sundays, we pitched and bounced in the rear of the army trucks taking us for rifle practice at various firing ranges. Lying prone and facing large bullseyes placed at distance, our growing arms quivered under the need to keep a steady aim. With a vicious recoil, the brass butt made any possibility of a steady shot nigh impossible, most of the bullets ending up in the stratosphere.

With burnished buttons, buffed up boots and battalion badges we paraded in all of our finery like the grand old Duke of York around the town's gradients. We formed a guard of honour for the Bishop on Confirmation Day. Each St. Patrick's Day parade, we stepped with purpose to signify our undying loyalty to Church and State.

Summer camp at Gormanston Military Barracks was for us boring and impecunious during the long school break, akin to a seaside holiday... with pay thrown in. The Barracks was situated on the sliver of Co. Meath shoreline, wedged between Co. Louth and Co. Dublin. Each dawn at reveille, we stirred sheepishly from a Nissan Hut dormitory for a wake-up of a drill and roll call. In the canteen we wolfed down greasy eggs, bacon and sausages, mounds of buttered bread all washed down by metal mugs of strong sweet tea. For a week long, we were shrieked at by intimidating N.C.O.'s. displaying maximum enthusiasm with minimum effort. Daytime duties were preoccupied by honing our skills against invasion by the Russian Bear. With our billets spick and span for daily inspection, we engaged in both weapons maintenance and rifle target practice. On alternate days, physical fitness instructors tried to turn us from teenage slouches into Celtic Warriors.

Evenings, all "dolled up and Brylcreemed", we decamped in throngs for the lure and bright lights of nearby towns. Drogheda was a large provincial town to the north, Butlin's Holiday Camp was a mere stone's throw away, and to the south nestling in north Co. Dublin, the village of Balbriggan lapped by the Irish Sea.

Drogheda, embedded into every schoolboy's history lesson, was where Oliver Cromwell, Lord Protector of England, during a countrywide rampage inflicted his puritanical zeal by slaughtering men, women and children. Drogheda's church, St. Peter's, displayed the venerated and mummified head of St. Oliver Plunkett, a Catholic cleric, hanged, drawn and quartered at Tyburn, now London's Marble Arch.

Away from our daytime onerous training to protect the Republic, the corner boys of Connolly's Corner and the Diamond now mingled with our local counterparts of Drogheda, where strategic observation posts were normally banks and where low lying window sills along the streets were polished by years of swaying arses.

On alternate evenings we headed for Balbriggan where the seafront lights swung in the tidal breeze. Another holiday camp at Skerries offered ballroom dancing, variety shows, talent competitions and quiz shows.

An added incentive for our youthful allegiance to "Saorstat Éireann" was the meagre annual monetary gratuity for services rendered. Saluting briskly before the Camp Paymaster seated at a table covered with legal tender and coins, two crisp £5 notes, and two £1 notes, plus a miscellany of silver and copper were slipped into an envelope and pressed into our grateful hands.

After an all too brief stint as custodians of the revolution, an undying allegiance to the tricolor and keeping the Kremlin at bay, most of us only stayed in the F.C.A. for a year or two. Because of the chronic nationwide unemployment, some boys from large poor families, whose seeds of a military career were sown in the F.C.A., crossed the border to the British Army recruitment centres in Omagh and Enniskillen, and some enrolled in the few remaining Irish regiments of the Inniskillings, the Royal Irish Rifles or the Irish Guards. After basic vigorous training at the hands of domineering Regimental Sergeant Majors, they were despatched to quell colonial rebellions in Aden, Cyprus and Kenya. Returning to Clones on annual leave, they stood out with their ramrod gait, tasteful dress code and clean cut personal grooming.

A few others fell under the spell of "Beau Geste" romanticism, and headed for Paris to join the "Légion Étrangère" France's own international army. Drawn from a motley band of misfits whose previous deeds, legal or otherwise, were never queried, they were trained up to highly disciplined regiments to police "Francophone" Africa and French Indo China.

However, the majority of us departed Erin's shores in droves for the gilded streets of London, the sidewalks of New York and the pavements of Sydney.

THE SASH

Each year, during late spring and early summer, the foreboding, ominous, hollow rhythms of the Lambeg drum reverberated across the evening ether and Protestant heartlands. A large piece of percussion, the Lambeg drum dwarfed its harnessed player. With a slackened skin for maximus hollow sound, it was beaten by the use of two slightly curved, long rectangular sticks. This tom tom, echoing over the twilight, was the wakeup call for the approaching marching season, the annual triumphal assertion of reformation domination.

The day itself, the 12th of July, would commemorate the victory of the Dutch Protestant king, William of Orange, over the Catholic Stewart, King James, at the Battle of the Boyne outside Drogheda in 1690.

Throughout the six counties, bands of loyal sons of Ulster, in sober suits, bowler hats and sash regalia, swaggered in step to shrill flute bands. One of the most divisive days of an uneasy daily co-existence, tension escalated by their insistence of marching through Catholic interface areas. Passing Catholic churches especially, their strutting became more strident, both flutes and fifes increasing in decibel.

Ironically, one of the most popular and peaceful 12th of July parades took place in the Donegal seaside resort of Rossnowlagh. Here, along its stunning beach, participants paraded in peace, picnicked from their cars parked along the compacted sand and patronised local hostelries who were more concerned with the boost in economy than religious ideology. Indeed, the spectre of grown men attired like the "McDougall flour man" doing their Grand Old Duke of York routine was much less of interest than overflowing tills.

This great annual gathering of Protestant solidarity also provided an opportunity of seeking out kindred spirit with a view to marriage. As Protestant numbers dwindled in the South, prospective brides and grooms crossed the divide to unite.

Whereas within the different sects of Protestantism, to select a Catholic soulmate, to have and to hold to this day forward, was anathema, taboo and beyond the pale. Marrying across the religious divide where Cupid shot his arrows in the wrong direction, a sombre future beckoned. Both boy and girl became social outcasts and disowned by both families. The Catholic Church would put even greater demands on a marriage, insisting that all offspring be baptised Catholic. The only options for most of these marriages were to be ostracised and the eventual emigration to the anonymity of the UK mainland.

"Compo"

Long before New York lawyers became "ambulance chasers" and turned personal injury claims into a corporate business, Monaghan folk in general, but Clones people in particular, the cute hoors, were way ahead of the game.

Intending claimants would hitch a lift from an unsuspecting motorist approaching an acute bend, hairpin or corkscrew, "and Monaghan had them in abundance". The skill involved exiting the decelerating vehicle with a manoeuvre once perfected gave the impression of inflicting maximum injury with minimal road contact. Others slid down ladders, skated on slippery floors or wobbled on their bicycles in front of vans, cars or lorries. This took place in the post-war era, where the x-ray was still in science fiction comics and deep pinpoint scanning was a "lightbulb moment on the far horizon".

On one occasion, one of the "poor victims" lying prone in the road, and feigning serious injury, was surrounded by the usual crowd of good Samaritans. In the panic, one do-gooder shouted, "Send for a priest," another, "Send for a doctor." The injured party, seemingly lying prone and lifeless, opened a semi-comatose eye and whispered, "Send for a solicitor."

Seeking maximum payouts, prime areas of the anatomy would be mainly hard tissue and orthopaedic. Shoulders, elbows, wrists, hips, knees and ankles were the favourite hunting ground for these gold diggers, but the top skeletal area wound would be the spine and lower lumbar region, where mobility aids could be most emphasised. The term "whiplash" entered the medical lexicon and legal briefs.

Compensation claims known colloquially as "compo" as regards car accidents involved the most bizarre litigation… babies sued their parents, husbands sued wives or vice versa, and brothers sued sisters. One of the most unorthodox cases with successful outcome which I recall from my teenage years was that of the "steel splinter"; a local railway employee alleged that a shard of metal had pierced his leg, entered his bloodstream, and was slowly edging towards his heart. It was travelling slow enough to afford him an 18-month Oscar performance of limping around the town, firstly on crutches, latterly on sticks with glacial movement. Finally getting his day in court in Dublin against the Great Northern Railway, the defending barrister quizzed the injured party as to how the offending metal penetrated his body. His retort, causing great mirth at the high court, was legendary... "Well, your Honour, I wasn't born with it, and I didn't swallow it!" On a subsequent day, confused by all the legal jargon swirling around, one witness testified as to seeing the victim leaving Monaghan Hospital supported by his wife. Raising a point of order to object and waving his crutch with indignation, he blurted out, "Your Honour, I support my wife like any other man."

A settlement having been adjudged in his favour and a large cheque looming, the victorious entourage returned to Clones for an evening of celebration. Packed into a local pub with much backslapping and drinks flowing freely, the steel shard nowhere near his heart, the successful litigant strolled manfully to the toilet, leaving his now redundant crutches leaning against the bar. The barman, in a withering Clones barb, beckoned him back and, pointing at the discarded mobility aids, retorted, "Where the fuck do you think this is, Lourdes?"

Football Days, "Catch and Kick"

Summer Sundays gave the town of Clones a much-needed commercial boost. St Tiernach's Gaelic football grounds, a spirit level field in a huddle of hills, was regarded throughout Ulster as a premier sporting venue. Long, wide and with a rich loam of rainfed grass, it gave a great spring to a football boot and a nice bounce to the ball. Gaelic games comprising of football, a hybrid cross between rugby and soccer, and hurling, a form of hockey on steroids, together with handball were the sporting embodiment of the Celtic warriors in Irish mythology.

Played at intercounty level nationwide, Gaelic football had special resonance in the six counties as a Catholic tribal badge. A totally amateur sport, its heroes came from every social hue. Doctors, dentists, farmers and tradesmen became legends beside humble labourers. The ultimate honour was to wear the county jersey. One of the country's greatest hurling heroes was Christy Ring of Cork whose day job was as a petroleum tanker driver. Each of the four provinces would produce an overall championship finalist; the successful provincial winners would become all-Ireland finalists. The contest itself played out on the hallowed turf of Dublin's Croke Park each September.

On match mornings of the Ulster finals in Clones, townspeople prepared for the oncoming windfall. Early cavalcades of cars filled every available parking space, and trains shuddering through the railway gates disgorged fans by the carriage load. Collection plates were swollen at last mass, pubs were filling up, and shops did a roaring trade in sweets, lollies and ice cream. In the halcyon days before health and safety and local authority planning, council houses along the route and adjacent to the stadium became cottage industries for the day, selling soft drinks and snacks. Ham sandwiches came in three varieties: ham only, ham and mustard or ham and tomato. Also concealed between wedges of buttered loaves were slices of limp orange and tasteless plastic cheese somehow manufactured from the luscious meadows of Ireland's golden vale. Street performers arrived like moths around candles. Travelling musicians, out of tune crooners and beggars hugged every street corner. One gentleman of Asian appearance drew a violin bow across the even end of a stainless-steel wood saw. Stripped to the waist for no apparent reason and in the midst of torrential downpours, he would quiver the pliable metal for a tremolo effect. Market traders from Dublin's Moore Street descended by the van load, selling apples, oranges, bananas and pears and every type of team bunting.

As kickoff time drew closer, Fermanagh Street emptied as the throng faced the daunting challenge of Church Hill, and most were equipped with liquid sustenance for the game's duration, pint bottles of Guinness or ale swaying in coat pockets.

The football ground itself was surrounded by a wooden fence. Pitchside seating consisted of low-level concrete slabs. Bounded on the main road by the clubhouse and dressing rooms, layered terracing sloped down to the pitchside. Most supporters would gather to stand on the "canon's hill" sweeping down from the parochial house and providing a panoramic view.

Toilet facilities were for the male majority and bladder-emptying only. Two temporary enclosed corrugated stockades were erected at the furthermost corners where, standing on wooden duckboards, the men sprayed the soil directly. In the summer heat, the air hung heavy with the aroma of recycled hops and at season's end, this grassy patch became a sward of enriched greenery. For the female minority, toilet facilities were provided in the now vacated team dressing rooms, with the air pungent from stale sweat and menthol embrocation.

To add to all of this aromatic mix, one complete side of the football field was the town's main rubbish dump in the midst of which, in his lone commentary box, Ireland's iconic radio broadcaster Michael O'Hehir described the proceedings above the noxious fumes of Clones waste. After the ritual ceremonies of both finalists marching a lap of honour behind a local band and the singing of the Irish national anthem, con brio, facing the national flag, battle commenced. Both teams comprised 15 players: a goalkeeper, three full-backs, three half-backs, two midfielders together with three half-forwards and three full-forwards. The ball could be caught, kicked and hand passed, but in no more than five steps. Possession could be maintained by means of "a solo run" covering territory rapidly by passing the ball from foot to fingers. With tall goalposts and a crossbar, rugby style, a score over was a point, denoted by a white flag, while a score underneath was a goal, equalling three points, signalled by a green flag. The ball, with inner tube inflated and of crude leather, was roughly stitched and laced. In the frequent showers and downpours, the ball transformed into a soggy lead balloon. Requiring skilful handling and with a bounce like a Barnes Wallis bouncing bomb on a German dam, as the game ebbed and flowed, banter between rival fans was good-natured, profane, humorous and civilised.

The game over in the late afternoon, the victorious and the vanquished trooped once more to the town's various watering holes to toast or commiserate. Heading homewards in a Clones twilight, ravenous and tanked-up stragglers crowded around the crubeen van. Crubeens are baked pigs' trotters and were manna from heaven, either to gnaw on the fatty gristle or suck the alcohol-absorbing marrow bone jelly. The exodus lasted long into the evening; railway carriages crammed like Japanese bullet trains shunted sedately towards the surrounding counties. Overloaded cars on sagging springs struggled around the town's hills.

In the fading light, we children descended like locusts to sift meticulously through a canopy of litter deposited by the departed multitude. With eagle eyes, we scavenged for pennies, sixpences, shillings and half-crowns peeping under empty cigarette packets. But the main object of our rummaging was to collect the horde of empty beer bottles scattered everywhere. These we loaded in large hessian bags and, groaning under the weight, we redeemed to the town's grateful publicans.

Postscript: Jemmy Greenan

Jemmy Greenan's knowledge of football was encyclopaedic; however, his own talent for the game was best described in Clones parlance as "he couldn't kick snow off a rope". Wherever 30 players lined up, Jemmy Greenan was sure to be on the sidelines, whether local inner street tussles, intertown games or intercounty rivalry.

Attending the all-Ireland final in Dublin each year, Jemmy would exit Croke Park just before the final whistle and returned to Clones post-haste. Here, outside his parent's modest terrace house in the middle of Fermanagh Street, an eager audience had already assembled.

Having already listened to the radio broadcast, they nevertheless awaited with bated breath for Jemmy's in-depth analysis.

Setting the scene of the pre-match rituals, the ball ceremoniously thrown in by a prince of the church, the game was now placed under a microscope; this was a commentary in motion. Swaying from left foot to right foot between the footpath and the street gully, Jemmy would occasionally pause for emphasis, ejecting a small ball of spittle from the narrowest gap of his top teeth. Holding his listeners spellbound, he reprised every catch, kick, foul and score and moment of high drama. He rated the performance of full-forwards, half-forwards, midfielders of the high breaking ball, half-backs, full-backs, hapless goalkeepers, fisticuffs and referees. Recalling in fine detail a moment of drama or controversy, Jemmy would get all exercised massaging testicles in clockwise rotation. One of the most attentive of the assembled crowd, Peter Fox, a small, squat coal delivery man, would simultaneously rub his "cojones" in an anti-clockwise spin.

If only Jemmy Greenan could have played football as well as his florid descriptions of high balls, lowballs, sideline balls, fisted balls, saved balls and rotating balls.

FAIR DAY

Clones Fair in its heyday was the premier agricultural market for Monaghan and the surrounding areas. Held on the last Thursday of each month, with its hustle and bustle, it afforded us children not only a day off school, but an extracurricular activity, a field trip without a field. Proceedings started at dawn, country folk arriving in dribs and drabs before the first Angelus bell. Farmers drove their livestock towards the town centre. Amidst the din of lowing cattle, squealing pigs, crowing cocks, bleating sheep and braying donkeys, cartwheels creaked below the clatter of grey Ferguson tractors.

Divided into sectors for each species on the Diamond, pigs' snouts protruded from canvas-covered carts while roosters flapped in cages.

On Cara Street, thoroughbreds, ponies, cobs and donkeys lined up for critical inspection. Arranged with an angled aspect, with front hooves on the pavement, hindquarters sloping to give the appearance of puissance, manes and tails swished, tackle jangled, and horseshoes clopped impatiently.

On the Fair Green, in Analore Street, cows, calves and bulls exhaled steam in the cold morning air, slithering in methane manure.

The pivotal element of each fair day were the buyers and sellers and wheeler dealers, known collectively as "daylin' men". They were most conspicuous by their unique attire: a brown suit was normally topped off by a soft brown hat. Trouser turnups were hygienically rolled up above manure-spattered calf-high laced brown boots. A gold pocket watch glistened on a chain looped through a waistcoat buttonhole. Their only tool of trade was an ashplant, a long wooden pole tapering downwards from a sturdy handle … its primary purpose was for poking and prodding each potential purchase. With their hats pulled forwards and downwards, their chins resting on flattened palms atop their poles, their eyes darting over every forelock and flank, hindquarter and hoof, their brains were doing permutations and weighing options.

To observe the art of the deal was pure street theatre. The opening chess move was to belittle the object of their interest. Obese sows and pigs were cynically dismissed as "Where's the bacon for the cabbage?" Beef-bloated bulls, having been extensively prodded, were accused of having "less meat than an Oxo cube". Sturdy muscular horses "couldn't pull the socks off a corpse". Pigs were scrutinised hanging by their tails, horses subject to dental inspections and sheep prodded for their wool density. Thus, the opening derisory offer was greeted with guffaws of incredulity and instantly rejected, the gulf between buyer and seller seemingly unbridgeable as rebuffed dealers dramatically walked away "insulted by their fair offer". As both buyers and sellers held their ground, enter stage left "the tangler". The tanglers were the middlemen of their day as deal breakers; they were masters of closing the bargain. Experts in guile, compromise and timing, they brought apparent rigid sides together. Egged on by vocal spectators, the deal was finally sealed amid much backslapping and spitting on hands. All involved would now retire to a nearby pub where the interlocutor would receive their due reward… "a luck penny".

As the buying and selling ebbed across the town, the local economy became a trickle down. With jangling pockets, taverns overflowed, the town's barbers, Papa Jenkins, John Brady and Benny Dunwoody, snipped, clipped and combed, "talking to the mirror" of late frosts, early cabbage, wet weather and drying turf. In the "salon de coiffure", women queued to sit under dome-shaped hairdryers, their hair clamped in curlers. For a hairdresser, now referred to as a "stylist", to be "late of Dublin" was something, but to have "late of London" swinging on a sign was the ultimate cachet. In drapery shops, men measured for suits, women perused the latest couture, twirling in front of swivelling mirrors. In shoe shops, as men shoehorned hard-wearing brogues and wellingtons, women teetered on high heels. Shop floors absorbed street dung with layers of straw. Chemist shops displayed their array of scents in miniature bottles with gold tops. Here, less was more. The more exclusive the brand, the more miniature the bottle. Here also, the dialect of rural Monaghan mangled the household names of "les hauts parfumiers parisiens". So, Dior became "dire", L'Oréal, "loreel", Yves Saint Laurent came out as "wives Saint Laurence". Givenchy rhymed with "McGlinchy", Estée Lauder was attempted with "S.T. louder" and Gucci rhymed with "lucky". As miniscule samples were transferred from finger to wrist, such was the appeal of any tincture with a

French name, horse's piss could have been bottled and sold as "Urine de Cheval".

At the last port of call, in grocery shops, brown-coated counter hands shouldered bags of flour, boxes of tea and rural kitchen condiments to homebound customers. Street entertainment abounded everywhere. Jugglers, tricksters and musicians jostled with merchants laying out their stock of all things agricultural. A regular wandering minstrel was one "Nobby Clarke". A native of Monaghan town, he plied his cabaret trade hitching lifts on every possible mode of transport. Once raven-haired, his wavy mop, now mottled grey, hung shoulder length in the style of "the redeemer" and crowned with a crumpled wide-brimmed hat. Stubble-chinned and exhibiting molar stumps top and bottom, Nobby crooned a never-ending monotone tune of mumbled lyrics. With the occasional whistling intermezzo, he would also execute a balletic sidestepping routine. At the end of each rendition, Nobby, with a bow and a flourish, skipped through the milling audience, his hat upturned in mendicant mode.

If the fair day was not a fair-weather day, the streets of Clones became a quagmire as animals left a trail of brown steaming purée. Cartwheels and tractor tyres wove out winding ruts, while wellingtons and dealer's boots stamped out hobnailed indentations. No Irish fair would ever be complete without the tinkers. A term of its day, it was widely accepted to describe the native Irish gypsies whose stock in trade was the making and mending of all things tin. With their brightly painted caravans and roadside encampments, they followed the Irish fair day calendar at a pace of one horsepower. As the menfolk tapped and turned domestic vessels, their wives, with bangled earrings, golden teeth and Galway shawl, foretold futures or sold sprigs of lucky heather. Nevertheless, a couple of traveller families would break away from this traditional craft to become successful horse dealers. Prominent of these were the Mahons from the west, who blazed the horseshoe trail. The patriarch of the clan, old man Mahon, cut a dash between blinkers, halters and bridles. With a wide-brimmed fedora hat, frock coat, breeches and riding boots, he had the innate nose for a bargain to equal any thoroughbred trainer or owner at Tattersalls in Newmarket. With no fixed abode and living on the verges, the Mahons bought and sold early, quickly offloading a lot of their unwanted stock to eager recipients.

Postscript: James Dillon

James Dillon represented County Monaghan as a TD (MP) in the mid-1950s. Of the pro-treaty Fine Gael Party, Dillon's political lineage would lie in the philosophy of freedom through constitutional means and political agitation as voiced from Charles Stewart Parnell through to John Redmond's Home Rule Party.

Promised a parliament in Dublin by Lloyd George as a sweetener for Irish military partition in the Great War, events were quickly overtaken by the 1916 rising. The small band of poets and artists in a failed coup were at first despised by the general populace as Irish regiments fought on the Western Front. Outraged by the summary execution of its naive leaders, public anger changed rapidly to overwhelming sympathy. A badly organised band of revolutionaries who gave the supreme sacrifice were now held as martyrs and heroes while victorious soldiers returning from the Somme were ostracised as pariahs.

James Dillon, a practising barrister at law, came from a dynasty of advocates. His was the rarified world of wigs and gowns, pink ribboned briefs and juris prudence. With a razor-sharp legal brain, he dissected complex briefs into simple layman's terms. A powerful orator, he could hold his audience enraptured whether in the courtroom, parliamentary chamber or the hustings.

Made Minister of Agriculture in a mid-1950s coalition government, Dillon was a Dublin-centric square peg in a rural round hole. It would be fair to say that neither his polished brogues nor pinstriped trouser bottoms ever encountered a farmyard gate or trod in farmyard odour, or as the French would put it, his manicured nails would rarely, if ever, "touche le derrière d'une vache".

Jimmy Dillon's most infamous ministerial howler was the "coals to Newcastle" scheme by importing cheap subsidised Danish butter into Ireland. Amid howls of derision, the poor layered their toast and sandwiches with what was forever known after as "Dillon's yellow butter".

On the campaign trail during one general election, James Dillon was addressing the electors of Clones, standing on the back of a flatbed lorry on the Diamond before a sizeable crowd of locals. As Dillon was in full rhetorical flow and speechifying best but pausing dramatically to emphasise a salient point, the vacuum was filled instantly by a heckler. A local farmer, egged on by sneering cynics and at the minister's ignorance at all things agricultural, shouted through cupped hands, "Jimmy Dillon, how many toes has a pig?" When the guffaws died down sufficiently, fixing his inquisitor with a withering glare normally reserved for witness box interrogation, there came the following rapier response: "Take off your shoes and you'll find out!"

GONE TO THE DOGS

Clones Greyhound Stadium was situated on a marshy strip running beside the main road to Monaghan town. It was about half a mile from the village's end, where the Monaghan brae sloped downward from the Diamond to intersect with the Jubilee Road, "...oops! Ninety-Eight Avenue". The venue itself was enclosed within a rectangular of corrugated fencing, now faded to a flakey green.

The irony of it all was that of the objects of a financial flutter, i.e., the racing dogs, very few were in fact grey. In fact, most displayed sleek tight coats of light brown, dark brown, black, brindle or a dappled mosaic of all.

Race meetings took place twice weekly on Tuesdays and Thursdays. As each contest lasted virtually seconds, an evening card of 10 or more sprints enticed punters in droves from the surrounding counties. The sport of artisans, its breeders, owners and trainers comprised of butchers, bakers, innkeepers, haberdashers and small tenant farmers.

Uniquely, men of the cloth were officially frowned upon by the mitres and croziers, who turned a Nelsonian blind eye to priestly participation. Most curates and canons went through the subterfuge of registering hound ownership in the names of their housekeepers or sacristans. But even the dogs in the street could spot the trackside charade of priests secreting their clerical collars underneath bellowing scarves. In such a Roman repressive republic, attendance at sporting events, both equine and canine, with a forlorn chance of beating the bookies, was both looked upon by church and state as a benign social outlet... "Better by far the clergy chasing dogs rather than women!"

Greyhound pups could be bred in a shed, bought and maintained cheaply and doubling both as a household pet and as a potential future champion. Their daily training regime for toning up tendons was at the end of a lead on any Free State road, street or boreen.

Meanwhile back in Clones, the sound echoing across the Monaghan Road marshes with the yelping of hounds restrained in holding kennels and ready for the off, a tinkling bell announced the arrival of the decoy hare, its tail rocking gently on the mini monorail.

As the trap gate sprung open, the chasing pack, lithe of limb and lung and in tight formation, nosed forward and backwards, the eventual winner edging it by a mere nostril.

Alternatively, away from the many dog tracks, dotted around provincial Ireland, a more insidious but quite legal form of the pursuit would render it almost a blood sport. Hare coursing took place in open countryside where enthusiastic foot followers witnessed the uncertain fate of a live hare released with something of a head start on the chasing dogs. Its survival technique of evasive manoeuvring and scurrying through thick thickets was pitted against the speed and agility of the chasing pack. The dogs in pursuit are now muzzled, unlike in the prehistoric era before animal rights, where the hapless hare, once cornered, met a gruesome end.

Vincent Clerkin, our next-door neighbour, shoemaker and the only male sibling of his seamstress mother and his dustman father Pat, kennelled a black retriever named "Bran" in his backyard, together with two wire-haired terriers, specifically trained for flushing out foxes from their lairs or badgers from their setts. On most weekends, feast days or holy days, Vincent set forth at sunrise, two bandoliers of brass-tipped cartridges crossing his torso and a broken double-barrelled shotgun draped over his arm. Stalking hill and dale with Bran his faithful dog doggedly at heel, his aim, if a bullseye, was hopefully to bag a brace of partridges or pheasants for the oven or hares for the jug.

Encouraged by the Department of Agriculture to reduce the surplus population of foxes and badgers, a bounty of five shillings was offered by presenting the tongue of either carcass.

And finally, to that great outdoor canine pastime, defined succinctly by Oscar Wilde as "the unspeakable in pursuit of the uneatable", strangely enough, fox hunting in Ireland was not only the preserve of the ground bourgeoisie and the nouveau riche, but also by the sans-culotte trailing reynard on foot. The remnant descendant of Cromwell's generals, abetted by the new Irish professional class, met up outside Palladian houses from Kildare to Galway and Meath to Tipperary. In their coats of Irish hunting green and brown velvet collars, they drunk their stirrup cups astride anxious mounts and packs of piebald beagles milling around, aping the antics of their counterparts in England's green and pleasant land where fox hunting was the sole preserve of dukes, earls and the establishment. Socialist and liberal peers in their jackets of cherry red left their principles behind as they gathered outside Cotswold village inns before crisscrossing the estates of Beauford, Devonshire and Bedford.

To paraphrase Winston Churchill… "Never was so much energy expended by both human, horse and hound to despatch an innocent creature in the most cruelest of ways."

Postscript: Other Leisurely Pursuits

The Lakeland counties of southwest Ulster, namely Fermanagh, Cavan and the "stony grey hills of Monaghan", provided the ideal conditions for rod, reel and gun, whether fly fishing on shallow weirs or tranquil loughs, with bobbing floats, past trailing bobbing boats and floating past bobbing coots and wild duck.

As with the sport of kings, stud farms of some acreage ran along a vein of luscious limestone grassland running through middle Ireland to the Golden Vale. Thin enriched loam together with a dietary supplement of high-grade oats would produce world-famous bloodstock, sturdy of both frame and fetlock. A multimillion-pound worldwide industry, horse racing was the reserve of the global elite, royalty, Arabian sheiks and the odd Irish syndicate in it "just for the crack".

Early morning exercise for thoroughbreds was spectacular, with the going dewy soft as both stable lads and mount were situated over the gallops against a breaking dawn sky.

MONKEY IN THE SADDLE

The brothers Tommy and Packie MacEntee resided on neighbouring farms just outside Clones. Scouring studs and stables countrywide, they purchased job lots of thoroughbred rejects, knackers, the old and infirm for export. Fed on lush grasslands on limestone soil, Irish horsemeat was a *"délicatesse gastronomique"* in France and Belgium, providing tasty and tender meat for the *"repas de soir"* dinner plates of Flanders and Normandy.

The other abiding equine pastime of the MacEntees was show jumping. Tommy's daughter Lulu, swarthy and with a Belgian mother, was an accomplished horse woman, whose sideboard brimmed with rosettes, cut crystal and trophies from gymkhanas nationwide.

But the real unsung hero of the Irish showground arena was their employee "Monkey McGovern", a tenant of Upper O'Neill Park, higher geographically but lower socially to the MacEntees. Monkey McGovern was a combination of farm labourer, stable lad and general factotum around the MacEntee farmyard. But once saddled, he was a master horse man, untrained but a natural. Possessing a telepathy between man and beast, he could, by the gentle tug of a rein, or nudge of a stirrup, coax clear air between hooves and high barred gates.

The pinnacle of the Irish show jumping calendar was the Royal Dublin Show taking place each August in fashionable Ballsbridge. Here, a council tenant from a Clones housing estate rubbed shoulders with Europe's eventing elite: the British, French, Dutch and Italians. Whereas the varying nationalities faced the rigours of gates, bars, moats and mounds in differing styles, this peasant in the sport of kings glided around the course with panache.

This was the golden era of Irish show jumpers. Iris Kellett, Dublin department store heiress on her elegant grey Galway Bay, Tommy Wade astride Dundrum, an oversized pony discovered in the shaft of a milk cart and with a heart larger than any of the obstacles he faced. The most coveted prize of the week was the prestigious Aga Khan Trophy.

An international team contest, the Irish jumping team of its day consisted solely of army officers, most prominent of which would have been Captain Ringrose. However, with his God-given talent, Monkey

McGovern should have been a shoo-in for the national team. However, his very basic education, scant literacy and numeracy would preclude him from the social skills required of a commissioned officer. Unbowed, Monkey would shove two fingers to the high society horsy set with his pièce de résistance. If successful on two separate mounts, he would do a lap of honour around the course, riding one and leading the other by the reins.

A Day in the Bog

During "The Emergency", and to contribute to the war effort, export of Britain's golden seams, black and shiny, hewn from the bowels of Yorkshire, Nottinghamshire, Derbyshire, Kent and Wales, ceased. To fill this fuel deficiency, the Irish government allotted portions of bog to all Irish citizens.

Peat bogs abound throughout the island and, for centuries, its turf was the staple fuel in every Irish cottage. Ireland's largest peat bog covered most of middle Ireland. To manufacture peat briquettes on an industrial scale, the government department "Bord na Móna" procured German-designed peat excavators which rolled backwards and forwards scraping the bog surface. The peat was then dehydrated and compressed forming peat briquettes. Belatedly after scientific evidence revealed the extensive damage caused to both its delicate ecosystem and its vital role as a carbon catcher, the bog of Ireland was allowed to return to its natural state.

When order was restored, and imports resumed, coal was delivered door to door in heavy hundred-weight hessian sacks from the back of a flatbed lorry. This anthracite depot business was run by local businessman Martin Carroll in an annexe of the railway goods yard. One of the delivery men, known to us as "The General", thought to have been a top-ranking officer in the War of Independence, was now doing the lowly work of humping coal to households by the sweat of his dusty brow.

However, my father, with a romantic attachment to the old ways of self-reliance, would continue to cut turf for the family home well into the 1950s. So, on a hoped-for dry day in May, my father, my brother John and I set out in the early dawn from home for Mr Morton's bog just over the border. Awaiting us and from a mile back the road was our very own turf cutting machine... Red Pat McDonald smoking a Woodbine cigarette. Son of Thrupenny bit McDonald, Red Pat was a small, wiry man with a low centre of gravity, a master of the sláin, the cutting spade. Topping up his UK dole money with a "wee bit of work of the side", and working cash in hand, Red Pat set to his task and worked steadily all day, fueled by two crates of Guinness and stopping only for a piss in the gorse. Using the sláin to maximum efficiency, he worked the double-edged implement to slice rectangular sodden peat from the ground, sliding each sod onto the bog surface, where we spaced them apart. Lunch was ham and cheese sandwiches packed by my mother. Tea was brewed from the cold clear limestone water of a nearby spring well and boiled on a Primus stove. Red Pat's work now complete, our work had just commenced. Thrice weekly we returned, turning the drying sods to the sun's rays. Now partially dry, they were stacked horizontally, leaning on each other in clumps of four or six for the breeze to play its part. Once completely dried out, the peat was now built in rectangular pyramids known as clamps. My father would draw curious onlookers as he built his clamp Kerry style, assembled in a circular fashion, almost resembling the beehive stone dwellings occupied by monastic hermits on bleak Atlantic outcrops.

At the rear of the bog, in close proximity to the Morton household, stood a slated stone wall cabin, almost totally obscured in a thicket of ivy and blackberry brambles. Its occupant was one Willie Gibson, a former man of the roads, but now slowed down by age and infirmity. He would occasionally tramp the road to Clones and on winter evenings would illuminate the road ahead by means of a candle encased in a brass lamp swaying atop a brush handle. Willie's abode, a grace and favour dwelling courtesy of Mr Morton's benevolence, was devoid of any creature comforts. His daily fare of potatoes, onions and carrots from the Morton garden, together with assorted meat trimmings donated freely by local butchers, simmered in a large enamel saucepan on an open hearth in a perpetual gruel. Repeatedly offered by my father and other bog users to "take a couple of sods for yourself, Willie", he repeatedly refused, instead foraging for twigs branches and fallen foliage to fuel his meagre fireplace. My father was in awe of this illiterate man's principled honesty… exclaiming, "An honest man is the noblest work of God."

The turf, dried and ready for use, now required attention to the next logistical process, that of transportation and storage. Once again, this is where PJ Galvin's useful network of "daycent" men came into play. Norman Douglas, his very name signalling a left footer, but married to a right footer, worked as a mechanic in Joe Dixon's garage, the local Ford dealer. Norman, gregarious, larger than life with dancing blue eyes and a nervous giggling laugh, was the very antithesis of the Dixon family. Religious fundamentalists, they lived in a local self-imposed purdah, and daily reading tranches of both the Old and New Testaments for relaxation and salvation. With the tipper lorry supplied by Mr Dixon and Norman at the wheel, and the Galvins squeezed into the cab, we eased gently across the subsiding surface. The operation required trips of three or four full loads. The final phase of the marshal plan jigsaw was storage. This was supplied either at a peppercorn rent or free of charge by Harry Kennedy, manager of Thompson's Poultry and Egg Store. Here, in the disused corner of a rusty shed, our bog bounty was tipped, stacked and stored.

Either I or my brother John were tasked with the daily grind of bringing the turf home. After filling a large sack full of turf, it was tied with string and laid horizontally between the V-frame of my sister Peggie's new Raleigh or the triangular frame of my father's patrol bike. Ahead lay the arduous chore of the push up Church Hill.

Postscript: A Smoother Road Ahead

However, things were about to change. In a fit of pique at Monaghan County Council's failure to implement a right to buy scheme for our house at O'Neill Park, we moved socially upward by going downhill to Fermanagh Terrace - known by all as the "Gullet".

Thankfully, the daily turf run was now on a plateau from Thompson's Store to our new residence at No Four which stood in the middle of a red brick terrace facing the railway station.

The penny looking down on the ha'penny, snooty residents of the Gullet were appalled at their bricks and mortar being compared to a gannet's digestive track.

Fermanagh Terrace – AKA "The Gullet"

With my mother's acquisition of an electric cooker and my father's advancing years, we finally succumbed to Martin Carroll's coal on the shoulders of "The General" whose only battle honour was to breathe the air of a free Ireland.

HURDY GURDY

Big Jim Culley was big... very big... very, very big. At around seven feet in his stocking soles, he was reputedly Ireland's tallest man. As an object of curiosity, he could have carved out a career as a circus or funfair freak. Instead, he was a freak with his own funfair.

With his unique physique as a young man, he tried his hand (literally) as a sporting lad under the Marquis of Queensbury rules. Jim Culley's boxing skills, however, were in inverse proportion to his reach. Slow, ungainly and leaden-footed, he prowled the ring with all the agility of a sloth. With a large protruding jaw, his "Achilles' heel", he was low-hanging fruit for any opponent agile enough to breach his reach. The zenith of his pugilistic career was a world championship bout against the then champion, Primo Carnera.

Defeated, but with sufficient purse money, Jim purchased his own compendium of fairground attractions which were painted in the usual gaudy tints of bright red, sky blue and lemon yellow.

Jim and his family travelled the high roads and bi-roads of Ireland in summer. In June/July, he pitched up in Clones for a two-week stay. The attractions were set up on a vacant site on the edge of McCurtain Street ringed by fairy lights flashing against the twilight sky. The lights and attractions were powered by a large throbbing diesel generator that could be heard all over town, competing with the blaring loudspeakers playing American pop music at nauseum including Slim Whitman's "China Doll", Elvis Presley's "Good Luck Charm" and Connie Francis' "Carolina Moon".

As the swing boats squeaked, chair-o-planes swayed, hobby horses pranced and bumper cars sparked static electric, the fairground's temporary fiscal drain strained the local economy. Shopping bills went unpaid, pub takings plummeted and church collections were low in coinage.

The biggest money spinner on site was the very unskilful game of pongo. A forerunner of bingo, participants sat around in rows forming a square. In the middle and at some distance was a low-level square frame honeycombed into numerous slots. Each player was given a softball to lob into a number corresponding to one on their small playing boards. The first to complete a vertical, horizontal or diagonal line claimed the prize money. Clones housewives rose to the bait and Big Jim Culley reeled them in. One jackpot game took place nightly, the prize money offered being the equivalent of a fortnight's wages.

The Culley summer living quarters comprised of a luxury "American trailer". Cream coloured with a light "aluminum" body, it featured a parlour, cooking galley, two bedrooms, shower and toilet. Airy and spacious, its many windows were festooned with tasselled net curtains, and four adjustable legs at each corner ensured spirit level stability. This stately home on wheels was a million lightyears away from its native equivalent. Irish caravans of their day were no more than plywood garden sheds on two wheels which bounced and swayed across the country's ramshackle roads.

Towing the Culley mobile home was another slice of "American pie" and Big Jim Culley's pride and joy: a 1957 Chevrolet Belmont, a coupe convertible in cherry red with cream upholstery. It was chrome-embellished from bonnet to boot, with whitewall tyres. Its rear wings tapered and trimmed, making it almost aerodynamic. Rear light clusters winked like Christmas trees. Underneath the "hood" purred a very responsive three-litre V8 engine. Exotic extras included automatic transmission, power steering and disc braking. We ogled at this mod con new world opulence in an island of black Ford Prefects, black Morris Minors, black Baby Austins and black VW Beetles. Such was his size, that even in the elongated footwell as he eased his bulk into the driving seat, Jim Culley's knees would snuggle just under the steering wheel.

Postscript: "The Milk of Human Kindness?"

Dairy pasteurisation was now the norm in the late 50s and the days of horse-drawn carts supplying warm sudsy bacterial milk from teat to teacup were numbered. Treated milk in crates of glass bottles with silver caps was now collected from creameries by vans and deposited on morning doorsteps. Mickey Connelly set up Clones' first milk delivery van.

Trying once to explain the health-giving properties of "past-your-eyes" (pasteurised) to an elderly widow in O'Neill Park, she fixed him with a whimsical glance and exclaimed, "God help your head, Mickey! I only want a wee drop for a cup of tae and not to wash in it!"

Mickey, lacking in basic social graces, at once curt, rough, blunt and abrasive, was certainly not known for his PR and sales skills. Conversation was of a monosyllabic discourse and fools were not suffered gladly. Rotund in face and body, his chubby cheeks a cardiovascular shade of puce purple, a withering look was recessed behind a pair of wire-rimmed "Himmler" spectacles.

A skilful billiard player in St Joseph's Hall, Mickey's party piece was his "philharmonic fart". Addressing a difficult canon or pot, his right leg supine along the table's edge, the performance commenced. With an auspicious audience, silhouetted in the gloom of the illuminated baize, abdominal gases escaped. Starting with a limp whisper, it rose in a crescendo of brass and percussion, fading away with an E flat.

Back on his daily milk round, Mickey expected his bills to be settled weekly and promptly. Neither was credit offered nor expected. When Big Jim Culley's caravan rolled into town, women in O'Neill Park, in tight curlers and plastic coats parading as dressing gowns, stood furtively in hallway shadows behind doors ajar, pleading with Mickey for a "wee bit of tick". Returning their bottles to their crates and with a suck-in sigh, his retort was the same to one and all... "You can fuck off and milk the hobby horses.'"

CARNIVAL!

Carnival! The very word resonates with "joie de vivre", extravagance, excess and overindulgence. Taking place annually across central and southern Catholic Europe, and by definition South America, its origins in the church calendar were the festivities proceeding the period of Lent and fast and abstinence.

In Venice, Europe's social elite disembarked from gilded gondolas masked, wigged and costumed to dance quadrilles in the Doge's Palace. Across Italy, Spain and Portugal, from village to town to city, pavement marquees doled out free fare amid boisterous bands and fado processions.

In Munich and Vienna, revellers abandoning Teutonic discipline traipsed through snowy streets to Fasching Balls. In New Orleans, at Mardi Gras, descendants of African slaves with trumpets, tambourines and trombones boogied on Bourbon Street. In Rio, Brazilians put the word carnal into carnival. For the weeks preceding Ash Wednesday, skimpily clad Brazilian beauties with boa feathers and plumed headdress sashayed on ostentatious floats to the throbbing sound of sambas and rumbas.

In Ireland, on the other hand, carnival would be more prosaic and less pulsating. Held each year in high summer, the Irish carnival was quite simply dancing removed from condensation-ridden halls to a condensation-ridden marquee. An event in a tent, the carnival took place in July/August and was organised as a fundraiser for the Gaelic Football Association. It was timed to maximise revenue from visitors and locals alike. We bored and restless scholars, long on holidays but short on funding, would congregate each evening on a grassy bank opposite to observe and ogle the female talent on show. What a beauty parade! Girls from surrounding counties exited from overladen cars; local girls, shop assistants and legal secretaries mingled with daughters of immigrant visiting relatives and speaking Glaswegian, Mancunian, Cockney or American. Teetering on high heels with heaving bosoms and fluffed-out skirts, the mating call of the summer was the swishing of voluptuous thighs encased in 15 denier nylons with suspender scaffolding. As they queued at the ticket box, our eyes, like organ stops, would trace the rear stocking seam line from ankle to arse.

As the band set up their equipment for the gig and for those still mastering their instruments, the marquee would reveal musical incompetence. The canvas, absorbing and deadening the sound, would expose every saxophone slip, guitar glitch and drum discord from which there was no hiding place.

To enforce entry by ticket, a tall picket fence surrounded the marquee, occasionally paroled by officials as twilight gave way to dusk. As the energy levels rose and the atmosphere turned feted, carnival air conditioning was primitive but instantaneous. By rolling up some of the tent's side flaps, a rush of noxious fumes escaped into the Clones night air to be replaced by the dewy aroma of drying hay and drying turf. This was our carpe diem moment. Moving at speed and stealth, we surreptitiously vaulted the perimeter fence and nonchalantly sidled up to mingle with the ticket-paying matrons.

Postscript: "The Pasodoble"

As the basic three-chord showband began to grow in confidence and musical dexterity, guitarists were emboldened to widen their fretwork network. Fingers picked out dominance, E flats and A majors, tremolos and riffs; some even experimented with Latin American beats, the samba, the rumba and the tango. If the tango, with its expansive strides and rigid head turning, was a challenge, the pasodoble was literally a step too far.

This classic bull fight manoeuvre transposed into crotchets and quavers with a staccato intro and pulsating tempo. Dancers in halls tried to master the footwork in a cross between a quickstep and a military two step. In fact, most people could neither spell it nor dance to it. Drummers were tasked to give the pasodoble the Iberian effect by shaking maracas or clicking castanets. Now, castanets, to most people, were what fishing trawlers from Castletownbere and Killybegs did in Atlantic waters.

Now it so happened that the proprietor of the carnival field was one Jonty Fairs. A rectangular flat meadow, it was sandwiched between the Jubilee Road and the railway goods yard. Jonty Fairs was Clones' equivalent of Wells Fargo - with his small horse-drawn box van he delivered post office parcels.

As the carnival drew to a close, one marquee was dismantled, only to be replaced a short time afterwards by a much larger canvas edifice… a circus tent. Duffy's Circus had arrived for its annual weeklong sojourn. With its typical entourage of exotic animals, clowns and acrobats, it departed its wintering quarters to traverse Ireland's highways and byways during late spring, summer and early autumn.

One of its most enduring popular acts were the prancing ponies. A troupe of piebalds of identical stature and markings were the equine equivalent of the "corps de ballet". Decked out in all their finery with groomed sheen coats, coiffured manes and tails, with a harness livery of polished leather and burnished brass and set off with feathered plumes, they promenaded proudly around the sawdust ring. On the ringmaster's command, they would, on raised hindquarters, execute a synchronised pirouette to the strains of the pasodoble. Whether through infirmity or old age, one of these strutting stars was offered annually to Jonty.

"What a comedown!" from a pampered life of privilege and audience agitation to delivering parcels around the rainy streets of Clones in the humble shafts of a parcel van. At the end of each working day, Jonty's pony and Duffy's Circus ex-tiller girl was allowed to graze and frolic in the carnival field.

However, in the cool of the evening with dancing in full swing, and a rising tempo at the other end of the field as the opening bars of the pasodoble drifted across the misty meadows, Jonty's retiree pony, now released from his postal duties, would prick up his ears, snort, neigh and do a perfect pas de deux.

And so it was, on a midsummer's night in a seething tent, in a grassy hollow in a border town a thousand miles from the nearest Spanish corrida, the only creature to choreograph the pasodoble perfectly was one infirm big top reject.

A CASSIDY ODYSSEY

As rural scholars with a large intake of farmers' sons, we town boys benefitted from long summer holidays, the harvest requiring all hands to the pumps. As soon as the schools closed, my mother would depart to South Donegal to steady the ship of the family boarding house and also to make it shipshape for the impending season.

Some weeks later, my heart pounding with excitement and assembling early morning on the Diamond, my Cinderella coach awaited. Transport to Bundoran was courtesy of Cassidy Buses, a small fleet of coaches based in Enniskillen, who plied their trade around the surrounding counties. In summer, they ran a daily "express" service between Clones and Bundoran. The Cassidy fleet was a motley collection of mostly ex-British army surplus stock. Newly liveried in light cream with chocolate brown contours, thereby avoiding any tribal sectarian colours, these vehicles were of spartan comforts, and more utility than luxury. Air conditioning was by way of rattling wind-up windows, seats vibrated in sync with the idling engine. With crash gearboxes, drivers worked their way through the gears by a combination of ear to clutch precision, but for a 10-year-old boy, this 60-mile trip was akin to a luxurious Greyhound Coach on Route 66. The ticket to ride to my Donegal Eldorado was a promissory note and read thus: "Dear Fred, please allow the bearer, my son, Jerry Galvin, passage to Bundoran... and oblige." The "Fred" in question was the conductor, Fred Doherty, an imposing figure and broad-shouldered son of Fermanagh. Sallow faced with an imposing "bird's nest" crop of fuzzy hair, Fred was Maurice Cassidy's multitasker from punching tickets, PR executive, tour guide and delivery man.

Departing the Diamond, Cassidy's liveried charabanc lurched and clattered across the border through the villages of Newtownbutler, Maguire's Bridge and Lisnaskea for a midday sojourn outside Cassidy's main office. Once again underway, the bus would hug the shoreline of Lough Erne on the portside of the river. Stops along the way became more frequent, making the term "express" a redundant adjective. Passengers also boarded randomly along the roadside while farms and homesteads were supplied with boxes of cheeping day-old chicks and vegetable seeds with various farm implements stacked in a corner in the rear. At each delivery point, up narrow laneways, Fred Doherty dallied with the recipients to discuss all the local news with "a wee cup of tae" or perhaps something a bit stronger.

Rising and falling, the Lough Shore Road became a succession of rolling switchback hills. The majestic Erne, dotted with its myriad of islands, now visible through a foliage of intertwined holly bushes and hazel trees. Bouncing along on the hollows, Cassidy's crowded coaches groaned under a rear suspension flattened by potholes or bog subsidence. Labouring on the gradient, the hilltops provided a panoramic vista across the north shore to the distant Donegal Hills shimmering in a blue haze. At Belleek, the River Erne ceased to be a British utility; at Ballyshannon, the River Erne, now the Assaroe waterfall, was harnessed, tumbling over German hydroelectric turbines to provide Donegal homesteads with electricity at the flick of a switch. Its energy now dissipated, the once mighty Erne became a sluggish stream flowing through the dunes of Tullaghan to mingle with the Atlantic rollers in Donegal Bay.

Grinding up the final gradient, the salt sea air wafting through wound-down windows, I got my first glimpse of the Atlantic Ocean shimmering in the distance.

Alighting at journey's end and thanking Mr Doherty profusely, I scampered post-haste to Antrim House and to the welcoming arms of my mother.

BUNDORAN

"Out from the cliffs, the seabirds fly,
on pinions that know no dropping.
Whilst out from the shore, with welcome charged,
a million waves come trooping."

Donegal Bay with Great Southern Hotel
and Bundoran Beach in the background

Bundoran is a seaside resort, nestled in the southwest corner of
Ulster and like its British counterparts of Brighton, Bournemouth and
Blackpool, its halcyon days extended from the late Victorian era to the
mid-1950s. The undulating Dartry Mountains, bookended by the table-
top Benbulben fairy mound, is a stunning backdrop overlooking
Donegal Bay. Benbulben, standing sentinel over the Ulster/Connacht
shoreline, is immersed in the Celtic folklore and mythology. Its facing
flank hugging the sea is a series of finger-like fissures, glacier gouged,
sweeping coastward across buttercup and daisy meadows to where a
ribbon of black basalt rock separates the land from sea. It runs from
Bundoran, past Tullaghan, whose sliver of land makes Leitrim a coastal
county. From here, it snakes past Mullaghmore, Lissadell, Maugherow
and Streedagh Strand, where in 1588, three Spanish galleons of

"*Los Invisibles*" were vanquished by the elements, blown ashore and splintered.

From June to September, its swollen seasonal population was a microcosm of Irish life on their "holldays". Trains would daily disgorge hordes of holiday makers and day trippers from inland towns and villages to brave the breakers on Bundoran's Mezzaluna Beach. Accommodation suited every pocket… country folk resided in B&Bs, and the petty bourgeoisie occupied the smaller hotels. A fair share of the visitors were Belfast Protestants availing of bargain basement prices and escaping the rigours of UK post-war rationing.

Dublin's elite motored down from the capital in their Humber Hawks, Rovers and Ford Zodiacs to reside at the impressive Great Northern Hotel. This striking edifice was stand-alone amidst a challenging 18-hole golf course skirting the Atlantic. Here the well-healed citizens of the professionals, business and academia whiled away leisure-filled days. Post-breakfast, doctors, dentists, directors and deans attired in cravats and blazers perused the morning papers. Lounging on leather-buttoned chesterfields, their spouses huddled in groups, gossiping around coffee tables. Mid-mornings were for the challenges of tees, bunker fairways and a links breeze, mixed foursomes or tennis doubles. Afternoons were time for gin and tonics, martinis, a rubber of bridge or a bracing clifftop constitutional. Evening dining was formal with a matching dress code. Guests, now suited and booted, dined off crisp table linen and with the finest bone china and silver service cutlery. The low hum of convivial conversation was intermingled with the chinking of wine glasses in one obtrusive corner. A local maestro, seated at a baby grand, tinkled Mozart and Chopin at "sotto voce".

The most raucous and extravagant input to the Bundoran economy was the Scottish invasion. Each year at the end of July, beginning of August (the Wake's Weeks), all Glasgow's factories and shipyards closed en masse. These workers, escaping a world of hard physical labours and rigid shift patterns, would turn the town into a tartan takeover. Their wallets flush with holiday pay, they proceeded to drink Bundoran dry. Boarding houses were at full capacity as whole families crowded into sparse space. From early morning to early evening, extended families turned Bundoran's horseshoe strand into a sardine tin. Faces pallid from tubercular tenements and factory furnaces now glowed crimson red from sun and sea. Gorbals grandparents, babysitting the wee bairns, splashed and paddled their shrieking charges in pools and shallows. Grandads sported the "Irish sombrero", a knotted handkerchief and trousers rolled up over the knees, and grandmas tucked bellowing dresses in their Victorian bloomers.

At the rear of the beach, Harrison's Amusement Arcade offered multiple attractions. Above the din of the various attractions, an organ rendition of the anniversary waltz ebbed and flowed on an Atlantic breeze, infused with the sweet and sickly smell of candy floss. In the penny arcade, slot machines devoured coppers in the vain hope of lining up three lemons, oranges, apples or bells in a row. Children popped up and down on separate hobby horses or car carousels, their mouths stained with ice cream, ice lollies or sticky rocks.

Alcohol consumption commenced early evening. Sunburnt faces, red raw, now glowed in the Bundoran twilight. Pubs and hotel lounges were in full tilt.

The bankers and barristers of Killiney and the professors of medicine and mediaeval history from Blackrock, together with their coiffured wives, enjoyed the bonhomie and conviviality in exclusive isolation. Conversely, on the lower social end, skilled metal machinists, factory hands and marine riveters from Clydeside downed copious pints of Guinness and "wee dram" chasers. Lounge bar tables sagged beneath beer mugs, tumblers and liquor thimbles. Conversation increased in decibels as the "Devil's buttermilk" seeped into bloodstreams with heads rolling amidst shrieking guffaws. Girls and boys scrubbed up with Brylcreem quiffs and ribboned ringlets played "ring-a-ring Rosie" around tables and chairs.

The town centre now reverberated to pub singalongs of Scottish favourites… "I Belong Tae Glasgae", "Just A Wee Deoch an Doris", "Loch Lomond", "The Tangle Road of the Isles", "Auld Lang Syne" and "Keep Right On to the End of the Road".

As the hostelries closed, the merry throng staggered homeward, linking each other for perpendicular support, and the night air hung heavy with the pungent smell of vinegar-laced fish and chips.

The early days of autumn saw the town revert to a sleepy coastal village save for the few discerning visitors who sought solitude in wind and wave. The last mass exodus, albeit with the longest journey ahead, were the swallows, who with their newly fledged young, deserted their craggy crevices and cliffside nesting holes for another year.

The mid-1960s would see the decline of the Irish seaside vacations as cheap charter travel and the lure of the Costa Brava, Costa Blanca and Costa del Sol guaranteed sundrenched holidays to a rain-drenched nation. The larger hotels would still remain economically viable venues for all-year-round activities such as conferences, weddings, christenings, funerals and musical concerts, mainly country and western. Smaller boarding houses and bed and breakfast accommodation now became empty echo chambers of an era long since gone.

The halcyon days of a Bundoran summer childhood and all things Atlantic would linger forever in the memory: scudding clouds and squalls; the salt-laden breeze; the lonesome keening of the seagulls; rolling white horses with spray bouncing off jagged cliffs; the raking sound of the ebbtide slushing over shingle; slithery seaweed, sun dried, brittle and black; the west-end swimming pool whose bracing waters were replenished twice daily by the pull of the moon; nuns holidaying from the capital and the country's Magdalene Laundries, who defrocked inside tubular towels to metamorphosise into Victorian bathing costumes; Richard Fitzgerald, piano accordionist, par excellence, and his cèilidh band accompanied by his sister Kathleen, a haunting chanteuse; and Pat Duffy, boat man, propelled to his lobster pots by a new-fangled pull-start twin-stroke outward motor, whose sister, Theresa, was also a nightingale balladeer.

Postscript: Parish Pump Commentary

In the midst of all this "holiday anarchy" was one oasis of calm… in a motorcar. My uncle Jack McGowan and his wife Minnie (my mother's sister) ran a rural retail outlet near the village of Garrison on the Fermanagh/Leitrim border. This crossroad shop, the Tesco of its day and an eclectic emporium, consisted of grocery, confectionery, hardware, animal feeds, seed vegetables, petrol pumps and funeral undertakers.

The McGowans, being childless, took under their wings a niece, Meg Maguire, as shop assistant and heir apparent. Her Maguire surname would eventually morph into Meg McGowan even though her married name was Meg Leonard. With her blue shop coat, a curl cascading impishly over her forehead, a dancing eye and a cheeky grin, Meg was a "natural" behind the counter. She was at her most caring while arranging funerals and at her most sensitive while handling bereaved relatives with her easygoing manner. She also trod the eggshells of the religious divide in such a febrile frontier area.

Each sunny summer Sunday, Meg would reverse the cherished black Austin car from its garage with a Fermanagh registration number of IL3006, destination Bundoran. It was a testament to the then paucity of car ownership and a luxury of the privileged few. Chrome headlights perched atop wide flanked mudguards, sweeping low as running boards beneath precision closing doors, and seats were hand-stitched brown leather. Wheels were silvery spokes with a shiny locking cap.

Proceeding the 20 or so miles to Bundoran at a sedate 30mph, she would park strategically at the junction of the main street and the promenade.

Dressed in their Sunday best, Jack, with a tailored suit and soft brown hat, puffed contentedly on his briar pipe while Minnie, with the latest fashionable millinery and brooch-embellished tweed jacket with a fox stole, cradled her packet of John Player cigarettes while sucking boiled sweets that she snagged from their shop's confectionary shelves.

Meg, behind the steering wheel, would provide a running commentary on all the "comings and goings" … family lineages were scrutinised, in-laws, cousins, nieces and nephews, courting couples, newlywed couples, expecting couples and drunken family feuds. With each nugget of news and gossip, Meg would clasp her interwoven hands, raise her eyes heavenwards and exclaim, "Well, I declare to God!"

Coming from a Fermanagh hamlet and with a parochial view of life, the McGowans were more than bemused by the antics of the Scottish "lads and lassies".

ANTRIM HOUSE

Away from the hotel grandeur, Bundoran's myriad of boarding houses shoehorned a year's enterprise into a 10-week summer period of frantic activity, and Antrim House was one such establishment.

Antrim House – from B&B to now advertising hoarding

So named because of my grandfather's Belfast origins, this end-of-terrace building was one of a conjoined pair. Constructed by my maternal grand-uncles, the Gormans, they were built to cash in on the burgeoning opportunities of Bundoran as a popular seaside resort.

These dwellings were situated at the western end of town on the seaward side of the main road to Sligo and sat precariously some 30 feet or so from the cliff edge at the rear, plunging to tidal rocks below.

Directly inside the front door, stage left and stage right, were two dining rooms, used alternatively for socialising and reading. Running off these two lounges were two separate bedrooms; this format was replicated on the floor above. A tiled hallway leading to the kitchen shared the staircase. Running along the first floor above the hall, kitchen and staff quarters, a slim corridor provided for more dormitory bedrooms, culminating in the "penthouse suite". This most desired room at the rear of the house, AKA "Over the Waves", offered a stunning view of Donegal Bay.

All bedrooms were supplied with regulation squeaking metal bedsteads, damp mattresses and rattling windows. Also, vying for space in each room were small, mirrored sideboards, containing a carbolic soap dish and elegant jugs and bowls. Hot water for shaving was supplied direct from the kitchen urn. One English visitor complaining of no bath or shower facilities was led by my uncle Jack to the rear of the house. Waving his arm towards the sweep of the ocean, he retorted, "Sir, how big a feckin' bath do you want?!"

Ablutions for all visitors was by way of a single toilet on the landing. This necessitated chamber pots under beds slopped out daily.

Staff accommodation for my mother, Kathleen and Lily, or the occasional seasonal maid, was a dormitory at the back of the kitchen. Directly behind the range and known as the "officer's mess", the constant heat from the oven rendered the room a sauna in summer but snug in winter.

In one-half of the basement, next to the back steps, was a room that functioned as a coal bunker otherwise known as "the linge." The sleeping quarters for me and my siblings were in a dungeon cellar in the other half of the basement. This damp, unlit storeroom was a repository for broken beds, torn mattresses and general bric-a-brac. In one corner stood a cast iron mangle with large wooden rollers swaying gently on an uneven floor. With flickering candles, we nightly tiptoed gingerly around this flotsam and jetsam to two double bedsteads, either side of a small apertured window. The pane, just about secured by weather-beaten putty, flopped incessantly in a worn frame. Dampness hung in the air, and the walls streamed condensation. Bedsheets were so saturated it was like sleeping between sheets of blotting paper.

Nevertheless, on starry moonlit nights, we peered from our beds at the sweeping beam of St John's lighthouse across the bay. Slumber came easy, through joie de vivre fatigue and the tidal lullaby lapping from the cliffs below.

Antrim House in my formative years was in the shaky hands of my two spinster aunts, Kathleen and Lily. As they were habitually totally unprepared for the impending invasion of guests and devoid of any planning skills, either my mother or my uncle Jack would take up residence each summer as a steady hand on the tiller.

Completely differing in every way, my two maiden aunts shared only a surname and a mutual loathing. In between the perpetual sniping and bickering, my mother would maintain an easy truce.

Kathleen was big, buxom, soft and tactile with an infectious laugh. Mentally fragile and highly strung, with features of a swarthy raven-haired Protestant, her gums long ago shrunk and petrified, she chattered through oversized dentures.

Lily by contrast was petite, slim, with auburn hair, cut in an elfin style, with rosy cheeks and twinkling eyes. Whereas Kathleen attired daily in size 16 cottony floral dresses, Lily had a penchant for tweed suits, polo jumpers, matching pearl earrings and necklaces. With a large strappy handbag, sensible shoes and lapels adorned with dainty enamelled brooches, Lily cut an elegant dash on her evening promenades.

As my mother assumed authority, both aunts had their own designated chores. In the antediluvian days before washing machines, Kathleen, as laundry mistress, was immersed to her elbows daily in a zinc bath of Sunlight soap suds, soaking, washing, scrubbing and rinsing the bed linen. Squeezed through a primitive mangle for its final cycle, sheets and pillowcases flapped and billowed in the breeze. Drying was completed on a wooden frame in the kitchen, lowered or raised to the ceiling on rope pulleys. Before ironing and storage, however, this crisp linen was lightly smoked from cigarette fumes.

Lily yet again by contrast was the pastry chef and dessert queen. Hers was the exclusive domain of flans, tarts, crumbles, buttery pastry, custard and whipped cream. Tinned peaches, pears, apricot, stewed apples, plums and gooseberries were decanted into Lily's pride and joy, an antique set of china pudding bowls with gilded rims, their bases depicting hunting scenes of English yeomanry, with the ultimate proof of provenance on the obverse side… made in Stoke.

In high summer, the Antrim House kitchen became a mini Dante's Inferno. On the hottest of days, a large cast metal range blazed away as my mother baked, boiled, braised, roasted or brewed endless cups of tea.

Daily indecision led to a daily crisis; forward planning was when the day's menu was decided at 9 o'clock instead of 10 o'clock in a fog of John Player fumes. Luckily for Antrim House, their supply chain was situated directly over the road. Pat Conlon's combined greengrocery and victuallers was a very convenient convenience store. His meat storage facility was a small meadow attached to the premises, where cows and sheep blissfully grazed unaware of their imminent transfer from field to fork. All purchases being on account, bills were settled at season's end.

Daily food fare for the guests was basic, wholesome and substantial. After a hearty cooked breakfast, guests departed for various morning activities, returning for a midday meal of roasts and stews with apple trimmings. Evening offerings were light snacks of sardines on toast, stuffed tomatoes or a ham salad. On Fridays, a fish day in Catholic Ireland, my mother would peer through the kitchen window at the fishing boats offloading on the quay behind the house. I would be despatched to collect the catch of the day, either herring, mackerel, pollock or whiting. These, my mother gutted, flattened, dusted with flour and pan fried, served with doorstep slices of soda bread.

After dinner, the house became silent as its guests departed to the town's evening entertainment venues and the Jordan women now relaxed after the rigours of the day. They then repaired to the small, secluded shingle and shell beach behind the boat quay for a reinvigorating swim.

Later, the guests would return, merry and mellow from pubs or concert halls, and congregate in the kitchen for a nightcap of biscuits, tea, coffee, Ovaltine or warm milk. Teacher, tailor, soldier, sailor, uninhibited by the hop and grape, crowded around the kitchen table, regaling the Jordan women with stories and tales from the border, Belfast, Glasgow and afar.

Sadly, unlike Bundoran's larger hotels that would survive as wedding, funeral and conference venues, the ultimate exodus of once loyal Irish/Scottish visitors to Benidorm and the Balearics would turn Antrim House and the town's other boarding houses into empty rooms, echoing the memories of yesteryear.

RELIGION

The Catholic Church in Ireland was entwined around every facet of life, like ivy around a tree trunk. From the foundation of the State, successive governments gifted to the Church its most sought-after prize, the subjugation of the education system from infancy to university which slanted all learning through the doctrinal prism of Rome.

Sacred Heart Church
Baptism, first communion, confirmation and altar boy

The liturgical year was punctuated by feast days, holy days, days of obligation, and days of abstinence. Morning, noon and evening, we school children incanted the Angelus by rote as the Angelus bell rang out from Sacred Heart Church. Evenings were for the family rosary, the holy hour, Stations of the Cross and the annual mission.

St Brigid's Day in February was celebrated by every schoolgirl weaving a cross from green rushes. Lent, the period of fast and abstinence, was broken by St Patrick's Day, and the month of May was dedicated to the Virgin Mary. In June, Corpus Christi involved a street procession, where under a gilded canopy, the priest held a jewel-encrusted monstrance containing the "Corpus Christi". Protestant neighbours along the route stood bemused in doorways, the word "idolatry" stamped invisibly on their foreheads.

Daily communicants crowded around weekend confessionals for sin-free continuity, others opted for the specific rewards of the "nine Fridays" whereby receiving the host on the first Friday of each successive month, entry to Heaven was guaranteed, bypassing the soul-cleansing torment of purgatory.

In summertime, Aer Lingus airlifted diocesan pilgrimages to the shrines of Europe… Lourdes, Fatima and Medjugorje. Coach loads of trippers headed for Knock, Ireland's own Marian Shrine. Hardier souls sailed to the island purgatory of Lough Derg in Donegal for a three-day vigil of prayer, silence and introspection.

On one particular diocesan pilgrimage from the west of Ireland, the bishop took pride of place just behind the cockpit, his corpulence straining his seatbelt. En route, the flight encountered quite shaky turbulence over the Bay of Biscay. A female senior citizen and first-time flyer became most agitated and, blessing herself, called out in panic, "Jesus, Mary and Joseph, we're all doomed!" Shaking with fear, she implored the pastoral shepherd, "Your grace! Your grace! For God's sake! Do something religious!" This he did. When calm was restored, he took up a collection!

And yet, in the midst of this overwhelming fervour, evocative childhood memories remain, recalling the serenity and tranquility of an Irish village church; the all-pervading aroma of candle wax, incense and floor polish; the sounds of everyday life recessed in the distance; dancing dust illuminated by the shafts of angled light through stained glass windows; the silence only broken by the whispered supplications of an elderly lady rising heavenward as she fingered her swaying pearl rosary beads.

THE MISSION/THE MISSIONS

If ever one word, in an Irish context, merely by its singular or plural would signify two ecclesiastical functions worlds apart, the mission would be very local and parochial and preaching to the converted. The missions were global and preaching to the yet to be converted.

The Mission

Each year around the end of April, beginning of May, with lengthening days, shortening nights, ascending sun and arriving swallows, all Irish parishes went through a spiritual spring clean. The resident curates would take their annual holidays to be replaced by firebrand preachers from various orders, parachuted in for two weeks. These Oblates, Redemptorists and Franciscan monks were tasked with jolting daily communicants and weekly mass goers out of torpor and lethargy. This intensive onslaught was the spiritual equivalent of Jesuit jump leads. Taking place over two weeks and in an evening setting, it was organised Islamic style with gender separation: women normally the first week and men the latter. Each evening, after preliminary devotions, celibate men in monastic habits or robes of the varying orders would ascend the pulpit and survey the fashion parade seated below him. Their preaching skills were honed from successive spring times on the road and their mastery of soaring dialogue, dramatic pause, bellicose, gesticulation or gentle persuasion held each congregation in rapt attention.

At this stage, during the women's week, we altar boys had to remove ourselves from the altar. This would ensure that our prepubescent ears were not assailed by anything pertaining to sex. Overcome with curiosity, we strained our ears behind the sacristy door in order to hear what we were forbidden to hear. As women were reminded of their marital obligations, wives were implored not to deny their husband's conjugal rights and meekly yield in the name of God. Also, that all babies were a gift from God and a new soul for mother church and that menstruating was in fact the womb weeping for a lost pregnancy. Being in close proximity to another jurisdiction where contraception was freely available, our intrepid unmarried Franciscan firebrand looked down on the fervent faces of fertile females, implored that their husbands desist from using "those dirty rubber things" from pagan England.

On each evening of the second week, it was the turn of the town's menfolk to have their feet held to the fire. Guided through a checklist of relevant commandments and amid vocal decibels, they were harangued about fatherly responsibilities as breadwinners, while the evils of gambling, drinking and infidelity rained down on bared heads. All this finger waving by celibate clerics cocooned in a cloistered life.

To capitalise on all this temporary evangelical fervour, two entrepreneurial ladies, a Mrs Rice and Mary Comiskey, would erect small marquee tents at both church gates. These were stocked with artefacts of miscellaneous religious regalia. Pious objects included framed pictures of saintly devotion, crucifixes, medallions, bibles and holy missals. There were statues of Jesus, the Virgin Mary in her mantle of blue, St Patrick in emerald green, St Brigid, the Pope and Padre Pio of stigmata fame. Jostling for space were St Francis of Assisi and blessed Martin de Porres... all made of plastic and all manufactured in Taiwan. Rosaries of every beaded colour glistened on chains, and for the Clones reborn, there were small wooden crosses containing a spy hole revealing the pilgrimage sites of Lourdes, Knock and Fatima. But the most must-have souvenir of all was a small dome-shaped and water-filled plastic container depicting various holy sites, which, when shaken vigorously, was engulfed in a blizzard of plastic snow.

Another popular icon that took pride of place on most Irish sideboards and was held in high devotion was the statue of the crowned Virgin Mary in billowing red robes holding the infant Jesus at waist level, known as the Child of Prague (pronounced Clones style as "vague"). One faithful devotee tried to buy one of these at Mary Comiskey's stall late in the day, only to be told, "No, we're completely sold out, but I have instead a wee cracked Jaysus, and you can have it for half price."

But the humblest item of all that cleared both tents was a simple wax candle. These were essential for the closing ceremonies of both weeks where the rejuvenated worshippers renewed their baptismal vows by repeating the liturgy of their godparents at the baptismal font.

With the end of the high-octane fortnight of ritual and renewal, and the departing whirlwind of Franciscans in brown habits, white cords and leather sandals, Clones parishioners returned to the torpor of the Catholic calendar where days, weeks and months were punctuated by church chimes, Angelus bell, funeral bell, wedding bell, morning and midday mass, rosary, novenas, holy hours, stations of the cross and street processions on high holy days.

Postscript: Ned McCooey

On the last evening of the mission came the final solemn ceremony of renewing baptismal vows. The men all standing as one, bathed in the soft light of each flickering candle held aloft, answered the command from the pulpit to renounce the Devil and all his works and "pomps" with a "sotto voce mumble" of "we do". The missioner, unimpressed, asked for an encore "fortissimo". Almost on cue, arriving late and swaying into the porch, came Ned McCooey, the local blacksmith. Soft-hatted with broad shoulders and even broader biceps, Ned was an even-tempered farrier who shod bad-tempered horses. His ears ringing to the rhythmic beating of hammer on anvil, his face pallid from the forge furnace and an occupational thirst from white hot metal, he arrived well loaded with the black stuff. Somewhat unsteady, his lips caked with congealed stout and a wee bit crooked and contrary, Ned was ready for Lucifer! As the dying incantation of the message for the fallen angel echoed above the nave and chancel... Ned bellowed, "We do, the no-good dirty bastard!"

The Missions

The missions, plural, was the exhortation of the risen Christ to his disciples secreted in the upper room in Jerusalem and recorded in the gospel of St Mark, chapter 16, verse 15: "Go forth I beseech you and preach to all nations, baptising them in the name of the Father, Son and Holy Spirit."

Following in the footstep of the Irish monks who fanned out all over Europe to rekindle religion and learning post the Dark Ages, newly consecrated ruddy-faced priests and nuns were now traversing the globe, and spreading the message of the risen Christ.

In the late 1940s and early 1950s, seminaries and religious colleges were brimming with young men and women destined for the "Diaspora of Divinity". The sheer number of differing orders were legion, each dedicated to a particular continent. From the favelas of Rio to the shanty towns of South Africa, from the tribal villages on the plains of Sub Sahara to the Pacific Islands and the paddy fields of Indo China. A couple of orders even had the temerity to reclaim the wayward adherents of the English reformation, led astray by the sexploits of Henry VIII.

These missionary orders varied from Franciscans, Passionists, Redemptorists, Oblates, White Fathers, Kiltegan Fathers and the "crème de la crème" Jesuits. Young would-be postulants had the pick of convent life from the Ursulines, Mothers of Mercy, Sisters of Mercy, Poor Clares and the Order of St Louis.

For these eager young men and women, cocooned hothouse plants in an Irish Catholic theocracy from baptism to final vows, and now parachuted into a Ugandan village or a Polynesian island, the culture shock must have been jaw dropping. As Celtic skin burned and blistered under tropical skies and mosquitos gorged on rich blood, their bodies which were more accustomed to the temperate Irish climate, wilted under the unrelenting sun.

If the British Empire left a legacy of law, order and administration, Irish missionaries would concentrate on matters both spiritual and educational. As well as the three Rs plus a fourth, religion, two more could be added: rebellion and revolution.

If this was the first generation of the world's poor to be enlightened beyond the village boundary, their teachers were the first generation of a new independent Ireland where nationalism and Catholicism were inseparable.

After daily lessons of sums, scribbling, spelling and scripture, wide-eyed scholars under a Sahel sky sat spellbound as priests and nuns enthralled them with Ireland's David and Goliath history. They must have had a hard time trying to visualise a small green, waterlogged island off northwest Europe, blood soaked from a 700-year old battle against their nearest neighbour, known as the "auld enemy".

As is wont in Irish culture, this long conflict of uprising and rebellion, battles and heroes, was immortalised in songs and ballads, ringing out across the centuries, including:

The 1798 Rebellion: "Boolavogue"
> At Boolavogue as the sun was setting
> On the bright May meadows of Shelmalier
> A rebel hand set the heather blazing
> And called the neighbours from far and near
> Then Father Murphy from old Kilcormac
> Stirred up the rocks, with a warning cry
> Arm. Arm. He cried. For I've come to lead you
> For Ireland's freedom we fight or die.

Dublin Uprising of 1803: "Bold Robert Emmet"
> The battle is over, the boys are defeated,
> Ireland is standing in darkness and gloom.
> We were neglected and cruelly treated,
> And I Robert Emmet will walk to my doom.

Chorus

> Bold Robert Emmet, the darling of Erin.
> Bold Robert Emmet, I'll die with a smile.
> Friends and companions so noble and daring,
> I'll lay down my life for the Emerald Isle.

The anthem of post-famine young Irelanders: "A Nation Once Again"
> When boyhood fire was in my blood
> I read of ancient freedom
> Of Greece and Rome that proudly stood
> 300 men and three men
> And yet I hope that I might see
> Our fetter's rent in twain
> An Ireland, long a province, be a nation once again.

The Manchester martyrs: "God Save Ireland"
> God save Ireland, say the heroes.
> God save Ireland, say us all.
> Whether on the scaffold high
> Or the battlefield we die,
> Oh, what matter if for Ireland be it all.

"The Bold Fenian Men"

> Adown by the Glenside I met a young woman
> A plucking young nettles she ne'er heard me coming.
> I listened a while to the song she was humming,
> Glory oh! Glory oh! To the bold Fenian men.
>
> When I was a young girl the sound of their drilling
> Awoke in the valley, the sound it was thrilling.
> Sure they loved dear old Ireland and to die they were willing,
> Glory oh! Glory oh! To the bold Fenian men.

The Easter Rising: "The Foggy Dew"

> As down the Glen one Easter morn
> To a city fair rode I.
> The armoured band of marching men
> In squadrons passed me by.
> No fife did hum, or battle drum did sound the dread tattoo,
> But the Angelus bell o'er the Liffey swell rang out in the foggy dew.
> Right proudly high o'er Dublin sky they hung out the flag of war.
> It was better to die 'neath an Irish sky than at Suvela or Sud-el-Bar
> And from the plains of Royal Meath
> Young men came hurrying through,
> As John Bull's sons with their long-ranged guns
> Sailed into the foggy dew.

"Kevin Barry"

> In Mountjoy jail one Monday morning high upon the gallows tree,
> Kevin Barry gave his young life for the cause of liberty.
> Just a lad of 18 summers yet there's no one can deny,
> As he walked to death that morning, he held his head on high.
>
> Proudly standing to attention as he bade his last farewell,
> To his broken-hearted mother whose sad grief no one can tell.
> For the cause he proudly cherished this sad parting had to be,
> Then to death he walked softly smiling, that old Ireland might be free.

These songs of freedom from the lips of Irish missionaries, of the first country to start the rot of the British Empire and sung to impressionable scholars in tribal villages, would be the seedcorn to inspire the Pan-African freedom movements of the mid-20th century. The sun was setting on the pink-coloured globe like dominoes. On well-manicured high commission lawns, the Union Jack was being lowered to the strains of a lone bugler. These would be replaced by a roll call of new black African leaders, educated by the Father O'Briens and the Sister O'Keefes.

Two Clones priests would minister to their flocks on opposite sides of the planet. Father Art McMahon, whose family shaped shovels and spades by a mill wheel, took his vows of ordination to a career below the 38th parallel. Home on a sabbatical, he enthralled a packed St Joseph's Hall with a movie of Far Eastern life, shot on a 35mm projector, which threw grainy technicolour images on a suspended bedsheet while describing a totally alien way of life. Here, smiling men and women with conical hats pushed labouring oxen through submerged paddy fields or worked backbreaking labour sewing or harvesting rice. As one local wit in the hall remarked, "All that for a rice pudding!"

In a preamble before the show, Fr McMahon also explained that part of the Korean culinary menu was the eating of spiced dogs. As gasps of horror swept across the assembled audience, someone else quipped, "They must be barking mad."

Father Clerkin supplied the most exotic pastoral care in the South Pacific Island of Fiji. His parish was the Shangri La archipelago of islands and atolls, with blinding white sands, swaying coconut palms and shoals of serried striped fish scurrying for shelter in coral reefs. As a missionary destination, converting the laid-back Fijians to the Church of Rome, this would seem to be a ministry made in heaven. However, for a celibate priest, confronted with stunning brown-skinned Polynesian beauties, flowers embedded in tight curls and neck garlands just covering their breasts, this must have strained Fr Clerkin's ordination vows to his limit

Arriving for holidays back to a windswept, rain-soaked Ireland, his white tropical suit and matching Panama hat was most conspicuous in a world of black clerical cloth. Residing with his brother Pat, our immediate neighbour, I was awarded the unique privilege as the altar boy next door to serve him at his daily mass. Prior to his departure, Fr Clerkin gave me a small purse containing assorted Fijian coinage as a souvenir and keepsake. Displaying my acquisition in the schoolyard would give me superior kudos. We called these coins polo mint money, having holes in the middle, and marveled how money from so far away bore the images of King George VI and his newly crowned daughter Elizabeth II.

True to their calling, the vast majority of priests and nuns would devote their lives to the spiritual and material welfare of the world's forgotten. Most would end their days and breathe their last in shanty towns in the shadow of Kilimanjaro or by the banks of the Limpopo River. Others would heed the overwhelming urge to return to the land of their birth and now advanced in years, they would see out their days in the various colleges from whence they set forth.

ROCK 'N' ROLL/SHOWBANDS

In the mid-1950s, a musical tsunami was rolling eastward across the Atlantic from the "Land of the Free and Home of the Brave", and what a roll it was... rock 'n' roll. Evolving from a fusion of jazz, blues and gospel, its instant success lay in its simplicity, three verses on three basic chords and for three minutes duration, played on electric guitars with decibel drumming. It also crossed the American racial divide. White all-American apple-pied, bobby-socked and crepe-soled rock stars... from Elvis, Ricky Nelson, Bobby Darin, Buddy Holly, Eddie Cochran to Connie Francis and Brenda Lee, shared the limelight with blacks singing their way out of the ghettos... Fats Domino, Little Richard, Chuck Berry, Tina Turner, Diana Ross, The Ronettes and the Four Tops.

In de Valera stultified Ireland, this was akin to a breath of fresh air. Radio Éireann (Irish radio) was almost the anglophone mouthpiece for Vatican radio. Programmes outdid each other for dullness... agricultural programmes, masses, rosaries and the Angelus bell. On sanctimonious Sundays, with comely maidens dancing at the crossroads, from thatched cottages dotted along the western seaboard, jigs, reels and hornpipes played on fiddles, flutes banjos and accordions pulsated across the airwaves into Bakelite valve radios from the Ring of Kerry to the Burren and from Connemara to the Donegal Rosses. Marathon Wagnerian and Brookner dirges were conducted by maestros with unpronounceable names. Luckily, living along the border afforded us the crystal-clear reception of the BBC signal overlap of the light programme and home service.

Teenage Ireland decamped en masse to the new kid on the block... Radio Luxembourg, situated in the mid-European principality. It was the first commercial pirate radio station beamed at the UK, at 208 metres at the medium wave; it was our pubescent lifeline, an unstopped menu of rock 'n' roll music. Derided by my father as that "feckin' auld boogie woogie", Ireland was just about on the edge of its broadcasting footprint, and the reception was atrocious. We listened avidly nightly, our ears pressed against the radio speaker. We twirled the station finder knob with all the finesse of a burglar on a combination lock as the reception ebbed, hissed and whistled.

As the jiving craze took hold, strict tempo, sit down dance orchestras and cèilidh bands playing in village halls were swept aside by the new musical hybrid combo... the Irish showband. Its repertoire was eclectic, a fusion of rock 'n' roll, ballroom, country and western and Irish rebel ballads. Because of its basic rhythmic structure, musical notation was an advantage but not a necessity. Redundant traditional musicians now transferred their skills to the latest craze. Fiddle players twanged electric guitars, flute and tin whistlers now forced their breath into trumpets, trombones or saxophones and drummers rolled to a new beat. With the chords E, D and G, and a couple of fret changes at their fingertips, farm labourers, postmen, mechanics and hewers of wood and drawers of water metamorphosised nightly into showband superstars. Of more importance than playing in tune and on time was sartorial elegance. Showband suits came in a garish variety of light blue, dark blue, royal blue, lime, lemon, emerald green or dark chocolate. Shirts were silky white with laced collars and ruffled cuffs; suit lapels were edged with beads or sequins. Ties and dickie bows gave way to Texas-style lace strings, held in place by a buffalo clasp. All this peacock finery was held aloft with crocodile shoes, buckled and buffed. These travelling troubadours also outdid each other with catchy names... The Royal, The Miami, The Capital, The Drifters, The Dixie Landers, The Clipper Carlton, The Cadettes, The Freshmen, The Mighty Avons, The Mainliners and The Big Four.

If their attire and guitars were all things modern, these new minstrels traversed the dance hall scene in challenging conditions. The then arterial road system, before the EU infrastructure largesse, was like driving along the Mongolian Silk Road, best described in Gaelic with the word "bohar", translated aptly as cow tracks. Puddled and potholed, they were maintained by a thin layer of tar and chippings clinging to subsidence, bogs and swamps.

Showband vehicles were basically commercial vans adapted for the job in hand. This conversion was the addition of some unsecured extra seating behind the driver, the remaining space for equipment storage where bodies jostled for space. Engines struggled under the extra weight, windscreen wipers in a rain swept country were sluggish and inefficient, washers and demisters were luxury accessories, headlights were penny candles on unlit roads. Shock absorbers and leaf springs were aided by over-inflated three-ply cord tyres, bouncing their way from Carrick-on-Shannon to Carrick-on-Suir, from Dungarvan to Dundalk, from Ballybunion to Ballyshannon. Covering these distances in such hazardous conditions required the stamina of a Monte Carlo rally driver.

Postscript: Slow Slow Quick Quick Slow

With the zenith of showbands came the demise of strict tempo ballroom orchestras. These 7- to 10-piece musicians, seated and reading sheet music from lecterns, were fast approaching their nadir. These big bands of Mick Delahunty, Maurice Mulcahy and the Clones contribution of the McMahon brothers and Dave Dixon, fronted by a Bing Crosby crooner, were yesterday's music. The foxtrot, quickstep, tangos, sambas and rumbas were now superseded by a non-contact body sport. It also happened that almost as a last hurrah, England's most famous orchestra of Victor Silvester was touring the Emerald Isle. A master craftsman on the maple floor, Silvester featured regularly on the BBC light programme with his famous catchphrase of "slow slow quick quick slow".

Pitching up in Belmullet, a village on the Erris Peninsula in west Mayo and on the edge of Western Europe, it was affectionately known to one and all as the next parish to America. Checking the hall's facilities before the evening bash, Silvester's pianist would insist, where possible, the provision of a grand piano – the existing piano forte on stage had all the look of a battered Welsh dresser, rocking gently on three castors, its wood veneer dull and in stripped layers. The white ivories, chipped and nicotine yellow, played just about in key. The pianist pointing out these shortcomings was assured by the hall caretaker that a replacement grand piano was on its way. As the hall filled up and the orchestra filled up, a shiny, more modern but upright piano now adorned the stage. "But you promised me a grand piano," the forlorn pianist sighed, chiding the janitor who replied thus: "That's the grandest piano in all of Mayo!"

COURTSHIP IN THE BOGS

To accommodate this burgeoning social revolution, cavernous "palais de danse" mushroomed across the length and breadth of the country. Parish halls, village halls, community halls and tin sheds became bleak and leaking collateral damage.

The Irish government, sensing a new revenue opportunity, decided to levy a tax on entry tickets, but leaving rural venues exempt. This resulted in the most garish ostentatious hoofing halls in the middle of the bogs; these neon-lit Taj Mahals stood out like beacons in a dusk countryside.

The buildings consisted of breeze block rectangular constructions built for maximum capacity with minimum fire and safety regulations. Crowding limits were non-existent in these swaying sardine tins. A front foyer contained the box office, toilets and cloakrooms leading to a shiny, slippery maple dance floor and stage. Ironically, for a country fueled by the hop and grape, no alcohol was served; instead, boys and girls sucked bottled minerals through regulation white straws. With the atmosphere already saturated with teenage testosterone and oestrogen, the Devil's buttermilk was surplus to requirements.

Decoration was minimal, walls were painted in yellows, creams or blues, air conditioning was unheard of, as was acoustics - this was a bonus for day job amateurs where bum notes and discord were lost in a cacophony of amplification and echo.

Erected in the middle of the Irish bogs, usually a short distance from the main road, accessing the concrete forecourt on rainy nights involved treading across a sodden quagmire. Girls in all their finery made the hazardous short trip in wellingtons, a high heel protruding under each arm.

When full to standing room only, these mega marriage bureaus turned into Dante's Inferno. As energy levels rose, so too did the temperature. Visibility became minimal through a fog of cigarette smoke, where a combination of perspiration from gyrating couples mingled with Old Spice aftershave and cheap perfume. All this evaporated and ran down the walls in rivulets. Brylcreem flowed like white lava down foreheads and across eyelids, likewise eyeliner over buttermilk cheeks. Lacquered beehive hairdos flopped limp in the humidity. Added to all this the overpowering smell of Jeyes Fluid disinfectant (the original eau de toilette).

Pre-dancing rituals were similar everywhere as girls assembled on one side of the floor, standing in small gossiping groups, with rampant bulls on the other. With the first drumroll, a stampede ensued towards the "meat rack", surging to seek out the prettiest girls. Plain and not-so-plain females were cast to one side, flotsam and jetsam in a sea of flailing arms.

How I envied the slick gyvers twirling their partners clockwise, now anticlockwise, changing hands, now left, now right and overhead twirls. Rhythmically challenged and possessing two left feet encased in diving boots, I could only look on with envy and await a slower-paced dance. In a sour grapes sort of way, gyving and twisting seemed like a total waste of time and energy. It defeated the object of getting up close and personal and a chance of a chat-up. Impressionable conversation for the short duration of the dance had to be succinct and convincing. The night's standard icebreakers were "Do you come here often?" … "There's a terrific crowd out here tonight" … "Where are you from?" … "Are you here on your holldays?"

The slow waltz was always the golden opportunity for the "dry ride", the closest thing to sex without penetration. As the lights dimmed and the tempo slowed, a balladeer on stage crooned a country western tearjerker lament of lost love, while the suspended revolving mirror ball, reflecting a kaleidoscopic beam, showered the heaving throng below in a dappled rainbow. The dry riders were now rising to the occasion. The object of this exercise was to hold your partner in a vice-like grip, hopefully cheek to cheek, while massaging your erect penis through underskirts and soft, alluring female flesh. As the hall reilluminated, dry riders could be easily spotted exhibiting their badge of honour: small patches of oozed semen staining the top left or right side of their zippers.

For those who subsequently courted and married and whose sperm reached its biological destination, Irish dance halls spawned the present generation who tripped the light fantastically in The Oyster in Limerick, The Las Vegas in Tipperary, The Cloudland in Roscommon, The Silver Slipper in Sligo, The Starlite in Monaghan or The Atlantic in Bundoran.

Postscript: "The Tihichin Beauties"

Two sisters from a remote home state of the Fermanagh/Tyrone county boundaries were known as the Tihichin Beauties and were the epitome of sexual innocence in a sexually repressive era. They cycled frequently to Clones dance halls trying to look older than their years; however, they weren't very successful as their facial makeup lacked some finesse. The pale Celtic colleens sported a mismatch of cosmetics highlighting faces clogged with putty face powder, lips smeared cherry red, and cheeks ruby rouged. They resembled for all the world like Chinese maidens painted on the side of Ming vases.

One night, as the dance was nearing its end, one of the innocents abroad exclaimed to the other sister, "Mary, there's going to be a ferocious fight here later on!" "How can you tell?" asked the other. "Well, every boy I danced with tonight had a wooden chair leg in one of his trouser pockets."

Do it, But You Mustn't Enjoy It

Sex in the land of my youth was like daylight... everywhere, but invisible. For a race of people so loquacious, who gave the term "blarney" and "gift of the gab" to the English language, any reference to reproduction brought any conversation to a juddering halt. Feet shuffled uneasily, throats cleared, and eyes darted downwards as the subject matter quickly changed. With a mixture of Victorian prurience and Catholic guilt, actions spoke louder than words.

All outward shows of physical attraction were frowned upon. Never once did I witness my parents exhibit even a kiss or a cuddle. From that I would surmise that in the marital bedroom, my parents never saw each other totally unclothed. We were the generations conceived in darkened bedrooms under layers of blankets; the end result, pregnancy, was almost a source of mortal shame. Women draped themselves in floral smocks of tent-size proportions, with each swelling trimester the greater the cover-up, shielded behind long loose-fitting overcoats trailing the ground. Nursing homes were places of purdah from which mothers miraculously reappeared with new life in swaying carry cots and a million lightyears away from the young mums of today, proudly displaying their trophy bumps under skimpy jeans and even skimpier t-shirts. In the eyes of a celibate hierarchy, reproduction was a messy, dirty animal act which required ceremonial cleansing. New mothers were required to kneel at the altar to have their sullied bodies repurified.

As boys and girls transitioned into puberty in ignorant bliss, all queries as to the mechanics of sex were met with a wall of silence. Boys with pimply faces, duck down beards and breaking voices wondered daily as they awoke to erect penises oozing a strange white creamy liquid. At least for us boys, some half-baked information was gleaned from older boys in the schoolyard.

As for the female side of reproduction, the mystery deepened. This was made more puzzling by the sight of used sanitary towels, crimson-stained mini hammocks floating, partly submerged in a Donegal shore rock pool.

But the greatest overarching influence of the Church of Rome in things moral and physical would be the notorious mid-1950s scandal of the "mother and child scheme". A newly elected coalition government had, as its Minister of Health, an actual "doctor".

Noel Browne, having qualified medically in Dublin, did his postgraduate training in the Middlesex Hospital in London's Fitzrovia as both doctor and political socialist. He was impressed by the founding principles of the fledgling National Health Service, i.e., free medical treatment for all at the point of need regardless of circumstance.

As Minister, he endeavoured to set up a limited equivalent in a poverty-stricken Ireland, his first priority to provide for all aspects of antenatal and post-natal care, thus ensuring safe deliveries and healthy babies.

The assembled celibate mitres and croziers meeting in conclave denounced it as a "sky falling in moment". This would lead to abortion, birth control, marital breakdown, spiritual and moral decay; necessitating the immediate need to draw up and enforce a homily of strong-worded condemnation to be read out across every Sunday pulpit. This was a direct challenge to a democratically elected government.

In an act of supreme hubris, the minister in question was summoned post-haste to the archbishop palace of one Dr Charles McQuaid, Bishop of Dublin, torch bearer for the Generalissimo Franco, who made Genghis Khan look like Mother Theresa. Seated in his study and requiring Dr Browne to stand before him like a recalcitrant schoolboy, he berated a democratically elected representative for overstepping his brief and straying into an exclusive ecclesiastical domain.

However, through a combination of the liberation of the swinging 60s, a television in every parlour and the successive scandals of paedophile priests and convent laundries and orphanages, one generation would clip the angelic wings of apostolic dominance, something 'perfidious Albion' repeatedly failed to achieve over many centuries.

No more would the curate or priest with biretta and breviary enquire unabashedly from newlyweds… "Any sign of a new soul for mother church yet?"

EMIGRATION AND RETURNING HOME

Emigration has been a scourge of Ireland, touching so many families and haunting this land for centuries. In my lifetime, from the Queen's coronation in 1953 to the end of the swinging 60s, Ireland witnessed an export boom as its surplus population was dumped in the lap of 'perfidious Albion'. Boats from Dublin, Galway and Cobh and planes from Dublin and Shannon transported a whole generation to England and America in search of employment. Mail boats from Dun Laoghaire to Fishguard and Holyhead, as well as cattle boats like the Princes Maud with its human cargo becoming extra freight, brought the Irish to England in droves.

My family was no different than so very many others who left this land in search of employment. As each one of us left home, our father advised us with the following pearl of departing wisdom: "Get yourself a secure permanent job with a regular income and a guaranteed pension" (which of us as teenagers ever contemplated getting old?!!!).

The Old Bog Road – a haunting lament for the scourge of emigration

My eldest sister Peggie was the first of us to join the exodus in 1956. Peggie first rented a room from my Uncle Tom and his wife Betty in Gypsy Hill, London. She worked for Dutch radio company Phillips & Mullard. After being chaperoned by her English cousins around the mecca dancehall circuit in London, she decided to try her luck in the "Land of the Free and Home of the Brave". She set her eyes on the

Statute of Liberty in 1965 and she embedded herself in Irish New York. In 1968 she married her husband Denis O'Shea, another emigrant from Ireland. A decade later, after heeding the primitive call to exiles, the couple returned to Ireland and moved to Kenmare near his family homestead by the Cork and Kerry mountains. Once home, they immersed themselves in a plethora of local activities: - Peggie joined the Volunteer Irish Civil Defence Corps.; and Denis joined the Kenmare Tidy Towns Committee. With his boundless enthusiasm and civic pride, Denis, along with Fr Murphy the local curate, and other local volunteers, Kenmare won the gold medal and coveted title of Irish Tidy Town of the Year in 2000.

My eldest brother John left Ireland in 1958. Taking my father's words to heart, he spent his entire career in the humdrum but gilt-edged world of banking. He first worked at the Bank of South Africa in King William Street, then westward to the Bank of America in Davies Street; and finally with Lombard North Central, the loans and financial branch of the Midlands Bank. It was here that he escaped a life of desk drudgery and worked as an internal auditor checking the contractual obligations of borrowers. His great boast from that job was that he was a frequent guest at the world's most bombed hotel... The Europa in Belfast.

Both he and I becoming divorced almost simultaneously, reverted to what we were as singletons, not only brothers but best friends. With our new-found freedoms of farting, burping and leaving the toilet seat aloft, suitably fortified with the "Devils Buttermilk", we became Irish balladeers. We travelled to and entertained in the most unlikely places – from an Iranian restaurant in Cairns, to a Chinese eatery in Brisbane, to singing "the Fields of Athenry" along Las Ramblas in Barcelona, and in taverns from Turkey to Tenerife.

After his retirement in 2000, he followed heart's desire and returned to Ireland to live in beautiful Killarney. After nine idyllic years living in Kerry, John sadly passed in 2012 after a three-year stalwart battle with leukemia.

As for my sister Eileen, she along with Peggie were boarders at the St. Louis Convent in Monaghan Town. Academically main stream, her true talents lay in music. A precocious violinist, at age 16 Eileen was leader of the convent orchestra performing yearly the operettas of Gilbert & Sullivan. Pitch perfect, her repertoire ranged from Mozart to

Molly Malone and from jazz to jigs and reels. Her prowess with bow and string didn't go unnoticed by Mr McCarney, the choirmaster of Sacred Heart Church who suggested to my father that she should audition for the Irish Radio Symphony Orchestra. However, my father did not agree, as his mantra in life was education, education, education. Disheartened, Eileen left college midstream to work as an assistant to a Clone's chemist for the princely sum of £1 per week.

During a failed IRA campaign in the mid-50s, the border areas were saturated with guards in the South and the RUC in the North. A young guard from Co. Kerry came 'a courtin' whether walking out on summer evenings or holding hands in the local cinema. Eileen was deeply traumatised and led a long life of depression after he chose another local girl as his bride.

Eileen moved to London in 1959. If the Emerald Isle is famous for its bonhomie, conviviality and 'Cead Mile Failté', Eileen was the very antithesis - ploughing a lone furrow after leaving Ireland.

Upon moving to London, Eileen's life changed little aside from constantly moving and crisscrossing from suburban bedsits in Bloomsbury to Hampstead, from Wandsworth Common to West Kensington, Ealing Broadway to West Ealing and then to South Ealing, using my taxi as a removals vehicle for her meagre belongings. I trudged up countless flights of stairs into bare landings where high ceilinged Victorian rooms were warmed by penny candle electric heaters.

Eileen eventually returned to Ireland around the millennium, moving to my mother's county of Donegal. After Peggie became a widow in 2009, she asked Eileen to move to Kenmare to be closer to her and for companionship.

Having lived a life like a ghost in the shadows, Eileen's passing in 2021 was just as unremarkable. In a society obsessed with death, where every funeral is a mini State event, her cortege consisted of a mere five foot followers.

It is interesting to note that even my father returned to Kerry in the end as it was his dying wish in 1967 to be buried in his beloved Ballybunion. He is now divided in death with my mother as she was buried in Clones after her death in 1976.

So it is in the Kingdom that the majority of the Monaghan Galvins will repose in their eternal rest.

AND FINALLY...

We are the rock 'n' roll generation who compressed a millennium of social, cultural and inventive revolution into one lifespan. Between us, my father and I would span three centuries. My parents would live through two world wars, from horse drawn carriages to internal combustion engines, and flimsy biplanes to commercial air travel. Born British, they would die Irish citizens.

As for us, we've gone from the man in the moon to a man on the moon, from valve radios to the internet, and from wind-up gramophones to instant music streaming. We were born before plastic, credit cards, ballpoint pens, freezers, microwaves and tumble dryers. We advanced from cooled pantries to fridges, metallic wardrobes only seen in American movies, from brooms to hoovers, and from fossil fuels to solar panels. To us, central heating was a coal-fired range or a turf hearth in the parlour. Air conditioning was an open window. A chip was a piece of wood or eaten with battered fish. Being resourceful was part of everyday post-war austerity. All food was "bubble and squeaked". All clothes were repaired and recycled, socks were darned, jumpers and pull-overs restitched, and hand-me-downs were what it said on the tin. The only things thrown away were cigarette butts. We got married first and then lived together (what a novel idea!). Conception was now controlled by contraception... from the rhythm method to the pill, from "plaisir d'amour" to pregnancy from a laboratory test tube. Being gay was to be the life and soul of the party, aids were time-saving kitchen gadgets, and tomes of dusty encyclopedias can now be accessed by the touch of a button on Google. "Fast food" was a boiled egg or a ham sandwich and a "big mac" was a large raincoat. Boys and girls courted before the idea of computer dating. Coffee made from chicory came in sauce-like bottles and both looked and tasted like treacle. Smoking cigarettes was chic, "grass" grew on lawns, "coke" was for fireplaces, "pot" was for stews and a "joint" was a Sunday roast.

In my lifetime, the world has changed at a dizzying pace, but at least I am still here in 2022!

CPSIA information can be obtained
at www.ICGtesting.com
Printed in the USA
LVHW032303101022
730380LV00003B/100

9 781803 811673